MUSIC ★ ICONS

JACKSON

LUKE CRAMPTON & DAFYDD REES
WITH WELLESLEY MARSH

TASCHEN

HONG KONG KÖLN LONDON LOS ANGELES MADRID PARIS TOKYO

CONTENTS

MICHAEL JACKSON: MAN IN THE MIRROR

MICHAEL JACKSON: DER MENSCH IM SPIEGEL

MICHAEL JACKSON: L'HOMME DANS LE MIROIR

MICHAEL JACKSON: MAN IN THE MIRROR

Three acts loom over all others in the pantheon of iconic pop music history: Elvis Presley, the Beatles—and Michael Jackson. Each was also the victim of immense celebrity, tragedy and early death. John Lennon was murdered at 40, Elvis left the building at 42 and Jackson self-destructed at 50. Arguably the greatest all-round entertainer of the modern era, Jackson embodied the paradox of extreme fame: a truly gifted singer, dancer and songwriter whose extraordinary talent was matched only by the loneliness, eccentricity and ego-mania of his isolated position atop popular culture. (Interestingly Jackson uniquely unites all three icons: he married Elvis' daughter and owned the Beatles' songwriting catalog.)

Born on August 29, 1958, Michael Joseph Jackson was raised in Gary, Indiana by an abusively strict father, Joseph and mother, Katherine. The seventh of nine siblings, Michael was a natural entertainer from a young age. Joining his brothers, Jermaine, Marlon, Tito and Jackie in the exuberant, R&B-influenced Jackson Brothers two years later (subsequently renamed the Jackson 5), the group, fronted by Michael and Jermaine, served a club apprenticeship around the Midwest from 1966-1968 when they were signed to Motown. Personally groomed by Motown founder, Berry Gordy, the group notched up five consecutive US No. 1 hits between 1969 and 1970, each hallmarked by Michael's unique treble vocals and dazzling, James Brown-influenced dance moves. (The group, abbreviated to the Jacksons from 1976, would eventually rack up 32 US single chart entries.) After the family relocated to Encino, California in 1970, Michael was simultaneously launched by Motown as a solo act the following year with the first of several ballads, *Got To Be There*. Rapidly becoming a worldwide teen pop idol, Jackson's childhood was placed on permanent hold as he was directed through a relentless schedule of recording and performing both solo and with his brothers.

Rolling though the mid-seventies on duty with the Jacksons, Michael reemerged as a solo act in 1979. Paired with veteran producer, Quincy Jones, the duo released a dance-fueled R&B/pop classic in the form of **Off The Wall** with Michael now launched as an "adult" performer. It was his union with Jones—over three albums in nine years—which catapulted Jackson to global idolatry, superstar duets, record-breaking sales, unmatched chart feats and multiple awards. Although he may remain an underrated songwriter who penned most of his own hits, it was the title track to *Thriller*, composed by British hit-maker, Rod Temperton, which forever changed both his world and ours. Having already pioneered the fields of pop choreography and music video with the chart-topping *Billie Jean* and *Beat It* (which, critically, became the first African-American videos to air on MTV) the premiere of the 14-minute mini-film "Thriller" became a worldwide prime-time television event which propelled Jackson's fame and wealth to historic levels. The sense of perfection he brought to his wildly popular concert tours only elevated his position as the (self-proclaimed) "King of Pop."

While his success in the 1980s is matched only by that of Elvis in the '50s and the Beatles in the '60s, Jackson never regained the artistic heights or credibility of his work with Jones (their creative union cannot be overstated). The last 15 years of his life became a procession of deserved awards and accolades (including a two-time induction into the Rock and Roll Hall of Fame), occasional recordings, illness, two disastrous marriages, three children (raised solely by him) and dozens of lawsuits, the most damaging of which centered around his predilection for spending time in the company of children. An unending target of the paparazzi and still beloved by a core of devoted fans worldwide, his well-documented eccentricity was an endless source of amusement, self-marketing, derision, concern and self-destruction.

Tortured by loneliness, obsessed with material consumption and image-management, his professional talent and success were accompanied by increasingly bizarre personal behavior. His humanitarian proclamations and charitable efforts were permanently overshadowed by his controversial obsession with youth—both his own and others. In attempting to be mysterious, androgynous and neither black nor white, Jackson ultimately declined into a sad world of unending plastic surgery, prescription drugs, chronic debt and self-delusion.

Irrespective of his mountain of controversy and intrigue, Jackson's combined abilities as a supreme vocalist, dance provocateur, songwriter, video-maker and live performer simply know no equal. As an entertainer he was, above all, a perfectionist. As a human being he was, above all, an imperfectionist—unable and unwilling to live a normal life. Perhaps more than any other icon, Jackson's music magically transcended race, geography, sex, genre, age and color—a remarkable achievement for a shy, troubled boy who never grew up. While his untimely death in June 2009 shook the world, it is Jackson's musical legacy which will rock the world for generations to come.

MICHAEL JACKSON: DER MENSCH IM SPIEGEL

Drei Namen überragen alle anderen Ikonen im Pantheon der Popmusik: Elvis Presley, die Beatles – und Michael Jackson. Allesamt wurden sie tragische Opfer einer enormen Prominenz und starben früh. John Lennon wurde mit 40 erschossen, Elvis trat mit 42 für immer von der Bühne ab, und Jackson hat sich schließlich mit 50 selbst zerstört. Als womöglich größter Allround-Unterhalter unserer Zeit verkörperte Jackson das Paradoxon extremen Ruhms: ein wahrhaft begabter Sänger, Tänzer und Songwriter, dessen außerordentliches Talent ebenso groß war wie seine Einsamkeit, seine Exzentrik und seine Egomanie in seiner isolierten Position an der Spitze der Popkultur.

Michael Joseph Jackson wurde am 29. August 1958 geboren und wuchs in Gary, Indiana bei seiner Mutter Katherine und seinem Vater Joseph auf, dessen Strenge an Brutalität grenzte. Als siebtes von neun Geschwistern hatte Michael von Kindesbeinen an ein natürliches Talent als Entertainer. Zwei Jahre später gesellte er sich zu seinen Brüdern Jermaine, Marlon, Tito und Jackie in der von Rhythm und Blues beeinflussten Gruppe Jackson Brothers (die daraufhin in Jackson 5 umbenannt wurde). Mit Michael und Jermaine als Frontsänger tingelte die Gruppe von 1966 bis 1968 durch die Clubs des Mittleren Westens, bevor sie beim Label Motown unter Vertrag genommen wurde. Unter der Ägide des Motown-Gründers Berry Gordy landete die Gruppe 1969 und 1970 hintereinander fünf Nummer-eins-Hits in den USA, die allesamt von Michaels einzigartiger Sopranstimme und den eindrucksvollen, von James Brown beeinflussten Tanznummern geprägt waren. (Die Gruppe, die sich ab 1976 nur noch Jacksons nannte, konnte letztendlich 32 Hits in den US-Single-Charts platzieren.)

Nachdem die Familie 1970 ins kalifornische Encino umgezogen war, brachte Motown Michael im nächsten Jahr mit der ersten von mehreren Balladen, *Got To Be There*, als Solonummer heraus. Mit dem raschen Aufstieg zum Teenager-Popidol in aller Welt war es endgültig um Jacksons eigene Kindheit geschehen, angesichts eines randvollen Terminkalenders mit Plattenaufnahmen und Auftritten, sowohl solo als auch mit seinen Brüdern.

Während er Mitte der 1970er Jahre noch seine Pflichten bei den Jacksons erfüllte, trat Michael 1979 wieder als Solokünstler ins Rampenlicht. Zusammen mit dem erfahrenen Produzenten Quincy Jones brachte er mit **Off The Wall** einen tanzorientierten R&B/Pop-Klassiker heraus, der den Startschuss für seine Karriere als „erwachsener" Künstler darstellte. Seine Zusammenarbeit mit Jones – drei Alben in neun Jahren – war die Initialzündung für weltweite Vergötterung, Superstar-Duette, Rekordumsätze, eine beispiellose Hitparadenbilanz und zahlreiche Preise. Jackson, der als Songwriter immer unterschätzt wurde, schrieb die meisten seiner Hits selbst, doch es war der von dem britischen Hitmacher Rod Temperton komponierte Titeltrack zu *Thriller*, der auf ewig Jacksons Welt und die seiner Fans veränderte. Nachdem er bereits mit den Top-Hits *Billie Jean* und *Beat It* Pionierleistungen auf dem Gebiet der Popchoreografie und des Musikvideos vollbracht hatte (es waren zudem die ersten Videos eines afroamerikanischen Künstlers, die auf MTV ausgestrahlt wurden), geriet die Uraufführung der vierzehnminütigen Filmsequenz „Thriller" zu einem weltweiten Fernsehereignis, das Jacksons Ruhm und Reichtum in historische Höhen schnellen ließ. Und das Höchstmaß an Perfektion, das er seinen umjubelten Konzerttourneen angedeihen ließ, steigerte nur noch seinen Ruf als (selbst ernannter) „King of Pop".

Sein Erfolg in den 1980er Jahren ist nur mit dem Elvis Presleys in den 1950er und dem der Beatles in den 1960er Jahren vergleichbar, doch Jackson erreichte nie wieder die künstlerischen Höhen oder die Glaubwürdigkeit jener Titel, die in Zusammenarbeit mit Jones entstanden waren, ein kreatives Bündnis, das gar nicht hoch genug bewertet werden kann. Die letzten 15 Jahre seines Lebens wurden zu einer Abfolge verdienter Auszeichnungen und Würdigungen (darunter die zweimalige Aufnahme in die Rock and Roll Hall of Fame), gelegentlicher Plattenaufnahmen, Erkrankungen, zweier katastrophaler Ehen, dreier Kinder (die er allein aufzog) und Dutzender Gerichtsverfahren, von denen sich die für ihn verhängnisvollsten um seine Neigung drehten, gerne Zeit mit Kindern zu verbringen. Unablässig wurde er von Paparazzi verfolgt und von einem harten Kern treuer Fans noch immer geliebt, während seine wohldokumentierte Exzentrik zu einem endlos sprudelnden Quell der Belustigung, der Selbstvermarktung, des Spotts, der Besorgnis und der Selbstzerstörung wurde.

Er war von Einsamkeit gequält, von Güterkonsum und Imagekontrolle besessen, und zu seinem beruflichen Talent und Erfolg gesellte sich ein zunehmend bizarres Verhalten im Privatleben. Seine philanthropischen Proklamationen und sein Engagement für wohltätige Zwecke wurden dauerhaft überschattet von seiner umstrittenen Fixiertheit auf Jugend – sowohl auf die eigene als auch die anderer. Im Bemühen, mysteriös, androgyn und weder schwarz noch weiß zu sein, verfiel er letztlich in eine traurige Welt endloser plastischer Chirurgie, verschreibungspflichtiger Medikamente, chronischer Verschuldung und Selbsttäuschung.

Unabhängig von allen Kontroversen und Intrigen war Michael Jackson ein alles überstrahlender Sänger, Tänzer, Songwriter, Video- und Livekünstler. Als Entertainer strebte er vor allem nach Vollkommenheit. Als Mensch war er alles andere als vollkommen: nicht fähig und nicht willens, ein normales Leben zu führen. Jacksons Musik überwand möglicherweise mehr noch als die anderer musikalischer Ikonen die Grenzen von Rasse, Herkunft, Geschlecht, Genre, Alter und Hautfarbe – eine beachtliche Leistung für einen schüchternen, problembeladenen Jungen, der niemals erwachsen werden konnte. Michael Jacksons vorzeitiger Tod im Juni 2009 erschütterte die Welt, sein musikalisches Erbe wird die Welt noch Generationen später in Begeisterung versetzen.

MICHAEL JACKSON: L'HOMME DANS LE MIROIR

Trois noms dominent tous les autres au panthéon de la musique pop : Elvis Presley, les Beatles – et Michael Jackson. Tous ont été les victimes d'une célébrité immense, de tragédies personnelles et d'une mort précoce. Elvis est parti à 42 ans, John Lennon a été assassiné à 40 ans, et Jackson a fini de s'autodétruire à 50 ans. Sans conteste l'artiste de divertissement le plus complet de l'ère moderne, Jackson a incarné la gloire dans tout son paradoxe : chanteur, danseur et compositeur exceptionnellement doué, son talent hors norme fut à la mesure de sa solitude, de son excentricité et d'une égomanie entretenue par son statut de roi de la culture populaire. (Il est d'ailleurs intéressant de rappeler que Jackson a combiné ces trois icônes, puisqu'il a épousé la fille du King et possédait le catalogue discographique des Beatles.)

Né le 29 août 1958, Michael Joseph Jackson est élevé à Gary, dans l'Indiana, par sa mère Katherine et un père à la sévérité abusive, Joseph. Septième de neuf enfants, Michael commence sa carrière très jeune. Il se joint à ses frères Jermaine, Marlon, Tito et Jackie au sein de l'exubérant groupe familial aux influences rhythm and blues, les Jackson Brothers, qui sera bientôt rebaptisé les Jackson 5. Avec Michael et Jermaine en vedettes, ils font leurs armes d'« entertainers » dans les clubs du Midwest entre 1966 et 1968, date à laquelle ils signent à la Motown. Pris en main personnellement par le fondateur de la maison Motown, Berry Gordy, les cinq frères accèdent à la première place des ventes américaines à cinq reprises entre 1969 et 1970. Chacun de ces titres mondialement célèbres est sublimé par la voix claire et pure de Michael et ses pas de danse éblouissants, inspirés par le jeu scénique de James Brown. (Le groupe, qui se fait appeler The Jacksons à partir de 1976, entrera pas moins de 32 fois au classement américain des 45 tours les plus vendus).

En 1970, la famille déménage à Encino, en Californie. L'année suivante, la Motown propose un contrat solo à Michael et il enregistre dans la foulée la première d'une série de ballades, *Got To Be There*. Jackson, qui devient très vite une idole pour les adolescents du monde entier, ne vit pas son enfance. Les jeux et le repos n'ont pas leur place dans son emploi du temps saturé de répétitions, d'enregistrements et de concerts, en solo ou avec ses frères.

Après un bref retour dans le giron des Jackson au milieu des années 1970, Michael reprend sa carrière solo en 1979. Il s'associe au magistral producteur Quincy Jones pour réaliser un album conçu pour la danse, **Off The Wall**, devenu un classique du mélange R&B/pop. Michael apparaît enfin comme un artiste «adulte». C'est cette collaboration avec Jones – de laquelle naîtront trois albums en neuf ans – qui propulse Jackson au rang d'idole internationale: il enchaîne les duos prestigieux, les ventes records et les récompenses. Ses talents de compositeur sont manifestes, même s'ils ont souvent été sous-estimés. Bien qu'il ait écrit la majorité de ses succès, c'est le titre éponyme de l'album **Thriller**, composé par le faiseur de tubes britanniques Rod Temperton, qui change à jamais son monde et le nôtre. Pionnier de la chorégraphie pop et du clip musical avec *Billie Jean* et *Beat It* (les premiers clips d'un artiste afro-américain diffusés sur MTV), Michael Jackson révolutionne une fois encore l'industrie musicale en diffusant en mondovision le court métrage de 14 minutes imaginé autour du titre «Thriller». Sa fortune et sa célébrité prennent alors des proportions inégalées. Le perfectionnisme avec lequel il prépare ses tournées au long cours ne fait que renforcer encore sa réputation de «Roi de la Pop» (autoproclamé).

Le succès qu'il rencontre dans les années 1980 n'est comparable qu'à celui que connurent Elvis, dans les années 1950, et les Beatles, la décennie suivante, pourtant Jackson n'atteindra plus les sommets qu'il foule avec Jones (on n'insistera jamais assez sur l'importance cruciale de cette alliance créatrice pour sa crédibilité artistique). Les quinze dernières années de sa vie sont faites d'une succession de récompenses, de prix et d'accolades mérités (notamment deux inscriptions au Rock and Roll Hall of Fame), de quelques enregistrements, de maladie, de deux mariages désastreux, de trois enfants (qu'il élève sans leurs mères) et de procès retentissants, dont le plus préjudiciable concerne sa prédilection pour la compagnie des enfants. Cible éternelle des paparazzis, toujours idolâtré par un noyau dur de fervents admirateurs dans le monde entier, son excentricité est passée au crible, devient une éternelle source de moquerie, mais aussi de promotion personnelle, de dérision et d'autodestruction.

Jackson est torturé par la solitude, fasciné par la consommation matérielle et la gestion de son image. Son talent et son succès s'accompagnent d'un comportement de plus en plus étrange. Ses prêches humanistes et ses actions charitables sont obscurcies par les soupçons concernant son obsession controversée pour les enfants – les siens et ceux des autres. À force de tenter d'être mystérieux, androgyne, ni blanc ni noir, Jackson a fini par se perdre dans un triste monde fait d'opérations de chirurgie esthétiques incessantes, de médicaments, d'endettement chronique et d'aveuglement.

Si l'on met de côté cette montagne de scandales et de disgrâces, les incroyables dons de chanteur, de compositeur, de danseur, de provocateur, de réalisateur et d'homme de scène de Michael Jackson sont sans égal. En tant qu'artiste, il était avant tout un perfectionniste. En tant qu'être humain, il était avant tout un «imperfectionniste», qui ne pouvait et ne voulait pas mener une vie normale. Davantage peut-être que toute autre icône moderne, Jackson a créé une musique qui transcende les frontières raciales, géographiques, sexuelles, d'âge et de couleur – un accomplissement remarquable pour un garçon timide et perturbé qui n'a jamais grandi. Sa mort prématurée, en juin 2009, a bouleversé le monde, mais l'héritage musical qu'il nous a laissé fera encore danser plusieurs générations.

2
CHRONOLOGY

CHRONOLOGIE
CHRONOLOGIE

THE EARLY YEARS

DIE FRÜHEN JAHRE

LES DÉBUTS

1963
Weaned on the music and stage presentation of Jackie Wilson and James Brown, Jackson is seen by his mother Katharine practising dance steps in front of the mirror having already seen him perform *Climb Every Mountain* for his kindergarten class the previous year. She and her husband Joe are keen to nurture and promote their offspring's musical ability. With Joe as manager, Michael will join four of his older brothers, Jackie, Tito, Jermaine and Marlon, to form the R&B-driven Jackson Five, also sometimes performing as the Ripples & Waves Plus Michael. With Michael as their lead vocalist, they win a succession of talent shows, their first "non-contest" performance being at the opening of a Big Top supermarket. A local fixture by 1965, they enter—and win—a local talent contest at Roosevelt High School in Gary, Indiana, performing the Temptations' *My Girl* in the summer of 1966. The group will spend the next two years honing their craft on the Midwestern club circuit with audiences increasingly dazzled by Michael's vocal ability and perfectly-timed dance moves.

Jackson ist mit der Musik und den Bühnenshows von Jackie Wilson und James Brown aufgewachsen und hatte bereits ein Jahr zuvor vor seiner Kindergartengruppe die Musicalnummer *Climb Every Mountain* zum Besten gegeben, als seine Mutter Katherine sah, wie er vor dem Spiegel Tanzschritte übte. Sie und ihr Ehemann Joe setzten alles daran, die musikalische Begabung ihres Nachwuchses zu pflegen und zu fördern. Mit Joe als Manager schloss sich Michael seinen älteren Brüdern Jackie, Tito, Jermaine und Marlon an, um die R&B-orientierte Gruppe Jackson Five zu bilden, die gelegentlich auch als Ripples & Waves Plus Michael auftrat. Mit Michael als Leadsänger gewann die Gruppe eine Reihe von Talentwettbewerben. Ihr erster Auftritt außerhalb eines solchen Wettbewerbs fand anlässlich der Eröffnung eines Big-Top-Supermarkts statt. Bis 1965 hatte sie sich in ihrer näheren Umgebung als feste Größe etabliert und gewann im Sommer 1966 einen lokalen Talentwettbewerb an der Roosevelt High School in Gary, Indiana, mit dem Temptations-Song *My Girl*. Im Verlauf der nächsten beiden Jahre bei Auftritten in den Clubs des Mittleren Westens feilte die Gruppe weiter an ihren Nummern, wobei sich das Publikum in zunehmendem Maße von Michaels stimmlichen Fähigkeiten und seinen perfekt abgestimmten Tanzschritten beeindruckt zeigte.

Katharine Jackson admire les progrès de son fils Michael, bercé par la musique et le jeu scénique de Jackie Wilson et de James Brown, qui répète sans relâche des pas de danse devant son miroir. L'année précédente, il a chanté *Climb Every Mountain* devant sa classe de maternelle. Elle et son mari Joe veillent à encourager et à faire fructifier les talents musicaux de leurs enfants. Avec son père pour manager, Michael se joint à quatre de ses grands frères (Jackie, Tito, Jermaine et Marlon) pour former les Jackson Five, groupe aux fortes influences rhythm and blues, d'abord lancé sous le nom de Ripples & Waves Plus Michael. Avec Michael en chanteur vedette, ils gagnent une série de radio-crochets. Ils se produisent pour la première fois « hors compétition » lors de l'inauguration d'un supermarché de la chaîne Big Top. En 1965, les frères Jackson sont déjà des célébrités locales. L'été 1966, ils remportent un concours organisé par le lycée Roosevelt de Gary (Indiana) avec une reprise du tube des Temptations, *My Girl*. Le groupe passe les deux années suivantes à faire ses armes dans les clubs du Midwest, devant un public de plus en plus ébloui par les capacités vocales de Michael et sa maîtrise des chorégraphies.

MONDAY, AUGUST 12, 1968
TO TUESDAY, AUGUST 27, 1968

Having won Amateur Night at New York's Apollo Theater in August 1967 and made their first recordings in October for Chicago's Steeltown label, the Jackson Five now perform a 15-date residency opening for Motown Records' act Bobby Taylor & the Vancouvers at the Regal Theater in Chicago. Taylor has become instrumental in the group signing to Motown, introducing them to label staffer Suzanne de Passe and Berry Gordy—who will modify the quintet's name to the Jackson 5. (Gladys Knight had earlier recommended the group to Gordy who was initially disinterested.)

Nachdem sie im August 1967 bereits die Amateur Night im New Yorker Apollo Theater gewonnen und im Oktober ihre erste Platte für das Chicagoer Steeltown-Label aufgenommen haben, treten die Jackson Five nun an 15 Tagen im Regal Theater von Chicago als Vorgruppe für Bobby Taylor & the Vancouvers auf, die bei Motown Records unter Vertrag stehen. Taylor nimmt entscheidenden Einfluss darauf, dass die Gruppe bei Motown unter Vertrag genommen wird, und stellt sie der Mitarbeiterin Suzanne de Passe und dem Gründer der Plattenfirma Berry Gordy vor, der den Namen des Quintetts zu Jackson 5 abändert. (Gladys Knight hatte die Gruppe bereits früher an Gordy weiterempfohlen, der sich anfänglich aber nicht interessiert zeigte.)

Sortis victorieux de l'Amateur Night à l'Apollo Theater de New York en août 1967, les frères Jackson ont fait leurs débuts en studio à Chicago en octobre pour le label Steeltown. Ils entament en août 1968 une série de 15 concerts en première partie de l'artiste de la Motown Bobby Taylor & the Vancouvers au Regal Theater de Chicago. Taylor contribue largement à la signature d'un contrat entre le groupe et sa mythique maison de disques en leur présentant Suzanne de Passe et Berry Gordy – qui rebaptisent le groupe les Jackson 5. (Gladys Knight avait déjà recommandé les cinq frères à Gordy, qui ne leur avait alors pas accordé d'intérêt.)

SATURDAY, OCTOBER 18, 1969

Relocated to Los Angeles, personally groomed by Berry Gordy and billed by the Motown publicity machine as the protégées of Diana Ross, the Jackson 5 make their network television debut on "Hollywood Palace."

In Los Angeles, unter der persönlichen Ägide von Berry Gordy und von der Motown-Werbemaschinerie als Schützlinge von Diana Ross angekündigt, treten die Jackson 5 zum ersten Mal im Network Television auf.

Installés à Los Angeles, confiés aux bons soins de Berry Gordy, de Diana Ross et de la machine promotionnelle implacable de la Motown, les Jackson 5 font leur première apparition à la télévision.

SATURDAY, JULY 1, 1972

While continuing parallel careers as a soloist and as a member of the Jackson 5 and with three solo Top 20 American hits already under his belt, Jackson sings his new single, *Ben* on "American Bandstand." Written by composer Walter Scharf and British lyricist Don Black as a love song from a young boy to a rat, for inclusion in the movie "Ben," it will give the 13-year-old singer his first chart-topper.

Während Jackson weiterhin parallel solo und als Mitglied der Jackson 5 auftritt und bereits drei Hits unter den US-amerikanischen Top 20 gelandet hat, stellt er seine neue Single *Ben* in der Fernsehsendung „American Bandstand" vor. Das Lied des Komponisten Walter Scharf und des britischen Songwriters Don Black für den Film „Ben" ist die Liebeserklärung eines Jungen an eine Ratte. Es bescherte dem Dreizehnjährigen seinen ersten Nummer-eins-Hit in den Charts.

Menant de front carrière solo et participation aux Jackson 5, alors qu'il a déjà propulsé trois titres dans le Top 20 américain, Jackson chante son dernier 45 tours en date, *Ben*, à l'émission « American Bandstand.» Composée par Walter Scharf et le parolier britannique Don Black, cette chanson d'amour d'un petit garçon à un rat, qui fait partie de la bande originale du film « Ben », offre au jeune artiste de 13 ans une première place en tête des ventes.

MONDAY, JUNE 30, 1975

A press conference is convened to announce the Jackson 5's new recording deal with Epic Records, effective from March 10, 1976—which signifies the end of their Motown deal. The group will discover that Berry Gordy had registered a patent on the name the Jackson 5 on March 30, 1972, which will result in the group name-changing to the Jacksons for Epic releases. (Michael will also sign a solo deal with the label.)

Auf einer Pressekonferenz verkünden die Jackson 5 ihre neue Zusammenarbeit mit Epic Records, am 10. März 1976 tritt der Vertrag in Kraft und setzt einen Schlussstrich unter die Zusammenarbeit mit Motown. Später stellt die Gruppe fest, dass Berry Gordy den Namen Jackson 5 am 30. März 1972 hatte schützen lassen, weshalb sich die Gruppe unter dem Epic-Label nun Jacksons nennen muss. (Michael schließt auch einen Solovertrag mit der neuen Plattenfirma ab.)

Une conférence de presse est convoquée pour annoncer la signature d'un contrat d'enregistrement entre les Jackson 5 et Epic Records, qui entrera en vigueur le 10 mars 1976 et mettra donc fin à leur collaboration avec la Motown. Les frères Jackson découvriront plus tard que Berry Gordy a acquis les droits d'utilisation exclusifs du nom Jackson 5 le 30 mars 1972, ce qui les oblige à changer de nom une fois encore : chez Epic, ils deviennent The Jacksons. (Michael signera aussi un contrat solo avec le label.)

WEDNESDAY, OCTOBER 25, 1978

"The Wiz", a movie version of the Broadway musical based on **The Wizard Of Oz**, opens in cinemas across the United States. Starring Diana Ross as Dorothy and featuring Jackson as the Scarecrow, the film loses more than $10 million for Motown and Universal. It does however mark the first occasion that Jackson—in his movie debut—meets Quincy Jones, who serves as the film's music producer.

„The Wiz", eine Verfilmung des Broadwaystücks nach dem Roman **The Wizard Of Oz** von Frank L. Baum, läuft in den amerikanischen Kinos an, mit Diana Ross als Dorothy und Michael Jackson bei seinem Filmdebüt in der Rolle der Vogelscheuche. Motown and Universal machen mit dem Film über zehn Millionen Dollar Verlust. Jackson lernt bei dieser Gelegenheit Quincy Jones, den Musikproduzenten des Films, kennen.

«Le Magicien», version filmée de la pièce à succès de Broadway «Le Magicien d'Oz», sort dans les salles américaines. Avec Diana Ross dans le rôle de Dorothy et Jackson en Épouvantail, le film fait perdre plus de dix millions de dollars à la Motown et à Universal. Il marque cependant une étape capitale dans la carrière de Michael Jackson, qui rencontre à cette occasion Quincy Jones, producteur de la bande originale.

SATURDAY, OCTOBER 13, 1979

In the midst of the Jacksons' "Destiny" tour, and performing in Rochester, New York, Michael Jackson scores his first American No. 1 in five years with the red-hot dance smash, *Don't Stop 'Til You Get Enough.* Released on July 28, the self-penned number, originally demoed at his 24-track home studio with brother Randy, is taken from **Off The Wall**, his second collaboration with Quincy Jones, which will eventually sell over ten million copies worldwide—much to the surprise of Epic who were resistant to the idea of the Jones/Jackson combination.

Während seiner „Destiny"-Tour bei einem Auftritt in Rochester, New York, landet Michael Jackson seinen ersten amerikanischen Nummer-eins-Hit in fünf Jahren mit der heißen Tanznummer *Don't Stop 'Til You Get Enough.* Das am 28. Juli veröffentlichte selbst geschriebene Stück, das er ursprünglich mit seinem Bruder Randy als Demo im heimischen Studio aufgenommen hat, ist eine Auskopplung aus **Off The Wall**, seinem zweiten Album in Zusammenarbeit mit Quincy Jones. Das Album verkauft sich schließlich weltweit über zehn Millionen Mal – zur großen Überraschung von Epic, hatte sich das Label doch gegen die Vorstellung einer Jones/Jackson-Kombination gesträubt.

En pleine tournée « Destiny » avec ses frères, Michael est à Rochester (État de New York) quand il apprend qu'il a atteint la tête du classement des meilleures ventes américaines pour la première fois depuis cinq ans avec le titre frénétique *Don't Stop 'Til You Get Enough.* Le morceau sorti le 28 juillet, composé et écrit par Michael Jackson et d'abord enregistré avec son frère Randy dans le studio 24-pistes qu'il a aménagé chez lui, est tiré de l'album **Off The Wall**, fruit de sa deuxième collaboration avec Quincy Jones. Le disque se vendra à plus de dix millions d'exemplaires dans le monde – à la grande surprise d'Epic, qui ne voyait pas d'un bon œil la collaboration Jones/Jackson.

THE 1980^S

DIE 1980ER

LES ANNÉES 1980

WEDNESDAY, FEBRUARY 27, 1980

Having picked up Favorite Male Artist, Soul/R&B, Favorite Album, Soul/R&B and Favorite Single, Soul/R&B categories at the seventh annual American Music Awards and Best Singing Group of the Year with the Jacksons at the 12th annual NAACP Image Awards, Jackson now wins Best R&B Vocal Performance, Male category for *Don't Stop 'Til You Get Enough* at the 22nd annual Grammy Awards.

Nachdem Jackson bereits die Preise „Favorite Male Artist, Soul/R&B", „Favorite Album, Soul/R&B" und „Favorite Single, Soul/R&B" bei der 7. Verleihung der American Music Awards und zusammen mit seinen Brüdern die Auszeichnung „Best Singing Group of the Year" bei der 12. Verleihung der NAACP Image Awards gewonnen hat, erhält er nun die Auszeichnung „Best R&B Vocal Performance" für *Don't Stop 'Til You Get Enough* bei der 22. Verleihung der Grammy Awards.

Alors qu'il a déjà été sacré Meilleur artiste masculin, Meilleur album et Meilleur extrait de l'année dans la catégorie Soul/R & B lors de la 7ᵉ cérémonie des American Music Awards, ainsi que celui de Meilleur groupe avec les Jacksons au cours de la 12ᵉ cérémonie des NAACP Image Awards, Jackson se voit remettre le Grammy Award de la Meilleure performance R & B masculine pour *Don't Stop 'Til You Get Enough*.

FRIDAY, JANUARY 30, 1981

Jackson once again wins the Favorite Male Artist, Soul/R&B and Favorite Album, Soul/R&B categories at the American Music Awards. Still pursuing a parallel group and solo career, he will embark on the group's "Triumph" tour later in the year. (He will collapse from exhaustion in New Orleans, Louisiana during the tour.)

Jackson erhält bei der Verleihung der American Music Awards erneut die Auszeichnung in den Kategorien „Favorite Male Artist, Soul/R&B" und „Favorite Album, Soul/R&B". Da er noch immer parallel seine Karriere als Solokünstler und Mitglied der Jacksons verfolgt, geht er noch im gleichen Jahr mit seinen Brüdern auf die „Triumph"-Tour, in deren Verlauf er in New Orleans, Louisiana, vor Erschöpfung zusammenbricht.

De retour aux American Music Awards, Jackson repart encore avec le titre de Meilleur artiste et celui du Meilleur album dans la catégorie Soul/R & B. Il se produit toujours avec ses frères parallèlement à sa carrière en solo. Cette année-là, il les suivra dans la tournée « Triumph ». (Il s'évanouira d'épuisement à La Nouvelle-Orléans.)

WEDNESDAY, APRIL 14, 1982
TO FRIDAY, APRIL 16, 1982

Following a Christmas Day telephone call to Paul McCartney suggesting they write and record together, the pair records the cut *The Girl Is Mine* at Westlake Studios in Los Angeles. This turns out to be the prelude to the recording of a new album, to be called **Thriller**. Produced in just eight weeks by Quincy Jones and engineered by Bruce Swedien, it will boast Jones' top flight session crew including Michael Boddicker, Paulinho da Costa, David Foster, Jerry Hey, James Ingram, Paul Jackson, Louis Johnson, Steve Lukather, David Paich, Greg Phillinganes, John Robinson and Jeff and Steve Porcaro.

Nach einem Telefonat mit Paul McCartney am Weihnachtstag 1981, in dem Jackson vorschlug, gemeinsam Stücke zu schreiben und aufzunehmen, produzieren die beiden *The Girl Is Mine* in den Westlake Studios in Los Angeles. Diese Aufnahme wird Auftakt zu einem neuen Album, das später den Titel **Thriller** erhält. Mit Quincy Jones als Produzent und Bruce Swedien als Toningenieur entsteht das Album in nur acht Wochen unter Mitwirkung von Jones' erstklassigen Studiomusikern, darunter Michael Boddicker, Paulinho da Costa, David Foster, Jerry Hey, James Ingram, Paul Jackson, Louis Johnson, Steve Lukather, David Paich, Greg Phillinganes, John Robinson sowie Jeff und Steve Porcaro.

Après une conversation téléphonique le jour de Noël 1981, au cours de laquelle Michael Jackson et Paul McCartney ont exprimé l'envie de travailler ensemble, les deux artistes se retrouvent au Westlake Studio de Los Angeles pour enregistrer *The Girl Is Mine*. Cette collaboration sert de prélude à l'enregistrement d'un nouvel album, **Thriller**. Produit en à peine huit semaines par Quincy Jones et confié aux oreilles expertes de l'ingénieur Bruce Swedien, il profite du talent des meilleurs musiciens de studio enrôlés par Jones, comme Michael Boddicker, Paulinho da Costa, David Foster, Jerry Hey, James Ingram, Paul Jackson, Louis Johnson, Steve Lukather, David Paich, Greg Phillinganes, John Robinson ou Jeff et Steve Porcaro.

WEDNESDAY, DECEMBER 1, 1982

Thriller is released. With demos originally recorded at his 24-track Encino home, some with British songwriter Rod Temperton present, the album, will break all sales records and become the most celebrated and successful chart album of all time. It includes four tracks written by Jackson, with the rest chosen from 600 songs submitted to Jones including the title cut penned by Temperton. It will sell over 50 million copies worldwide and hit No. 1 in every Western country, including the United Kingdom and the United States, spending a record 37 weeks in pole position in the latter. It will also yield an unprecedented seven Top 10 American hit singles. It will sell over one million copies in Los Angeles alone and will receive a record 12 Grammy nominations. *Thriller*'s full sales potential won't be fully realized until the release of its second single, *Billie Jean*.

Thriller wird veröffentlicht. Mit Demo-Aufnahmen, die ursprünglich teilweise in Anwesenheit des britischen Songwriters Rod Temperton abgemischt worden sind, bricht das Album sämtliche Verkaufsrekorde und wird zum erfolgreichsten Chart-Album aller Zeiten. Es enthält vier von Jackson geschriebene Stücke, während der Rest aus 600 Songs ausgesucht wurde, darunter auch der Titeltrack aus der Feder Tempertons. Weltweit werden über 50 Millionen Exemplare verkauft, und in der westlichen Welt landet das Album an der Spitze der Charts – so auch in Großbritannien und in den USA, wo es mit 37 Wochen in der Pole-Position sämtliche Rekorde bricht. Beispiellos ist auch die Zahl von sieben Single-Auskopplungen, die unter die Top 10 der US-amerikanischen Charts kommen. Das Album erhält erstmalig in der Geschichte zwölf Grammy-Nominierungen. Das ganze Potenzial von *Thriller* offenbart sich aber erst mit der zweiten Single-Auskopplung, *Billie Jean*.

Sortie de *Thriller*. Jackson a réalisé les bandes démos dans sa maison, à Encino, parfois en présence du compositeur Rod Temperton. L'album bat tous les records de ventes et devient le plus populaire de tous les temps. Il compte quatre titres écrits par Jackson ; les autres ont été choisis parmi les 600 chansons présentées à Jones, où figurait notamment le trésor composé par Temperton qui donnera son titre à l'album. Il se vendra à plus de 50 millions d'exemplaires dans le monde et atteindra la première place des ventes dans tous les pays occidentaux, y compris en Grande-Bretagne et aux États-Unis, où il passera 37 semaines en première place, un record. Il reçoit pas moins de douze nominations aux Grammys. L'album n'atteint tout son potentiel qu'après la sortie du deuxième 45 tours, *Billie Jean*.

SATURDAY, MARCH 5, 1983

The Jackson-penned, irresistible pop/dance radio smash *Billie Jean* hits No. 1 in the United States. It will stay there for seven weeks, and coincide for one week with its British No. 1 position. Having entered the American chart in January, it transforms the fortunes of **Thriller**, Jackson's career, the financial status of Epic Records and the fabric of modern music itself. Only when it hits No. 1 does MTV, previously reluctant to air "black videos," begin showing the *Billie Jean* clip (relenting only after a threatened service boycott by CBS.) Featuring self-choreographed dance steps, the visuals combine with audio innovation to provide what many critics regard as the perfect modern-single project. In contrast to future recording, Jackson's vocals for *Billie Jean* were made in one take, and feature an uncredited Lyricon solo by Tom Scott.

Der unwiderstehliche Pop/Dance-Radiohit *Billie Jean* aus Jacksons eigener Feder erreicht die Spitze der US-Charts, wo er sieben Wochen lang bleiben wird, eine Woche lang überschneidet sich diese Spitzenposition sogar mit der Top-Platzierung in den britischen Charts. Dieser Song veränderte nachhaltig das Schicksal von **Thriller**, Jacksons Karriere, die Finanzen von Epic Records und die Grundfesten der modernen Musik insgesamt. Erst nachdem der Song die Spitzenposition

erreicht hat, beginnt der Sender MTV, der zuvor nur widerwillig „schwarze Videos" gezeigt hatte, den Clip zu *Billie Jean* auszustrahlen (und auch das erst, nachdem der Chef der Plattenfirma CBS Records MTV mit Boykott gedroht hat). Viele Kritiker sehen in der Kombination der eigenständig choreografierten Tanzschritte mit Innovationen in der Audiotechnik ein perfektes Beispiel für die moderne Single.

L'irrésistible tube pop/dance *Billie Jean*, qui inonde les radios, monte en première place des ventes américaines. Il la conserve sept semaines. Entré dans le classement américain en janvier, il modifie en profondeur le destin de l'album **Thriller**, la carrière de Jackson, les finances d'Epic Records et la nature même de la musique moderne. Ce n'est que lorsqu'il atteint la pole position sur le marché américain que MTV, jusqu'ici réticente à l'idée de diffuser des clips «noirs», commence à passer celui de *Billie Jean* (la chaîne musicale cède en fait sous la menace de boycott de CBS Records). Les pas de danse créés par l'artiste, alliés aux effets visuels et innovations sonores et au solo de l'arrangeur Tom Scott au lyricon, constituent ce que de nombreux critiques considèrent comme le single parfait. Fait rare dans la discographie de Jackson, sur *Billie Jean*, sa voix a été enregistrée en une seule prise.

FRIDAY, MARCH 25, 1983

Jackson performs both solo and with his brothers for the "25 Years Of Motown" anniversary spectacular at the Civic Center, Los Angeles. When the show airs as "Motown 25: Yesterday, Today, Forever," Jackson's ground-breaking choreography, toe-tipping, hat-tossing performance will prove to be a defining moment in American pop culture. The show will win an Emmy award for Outstanding Variety, Music, or Comedy Program in September.

Für das Jubiläumsspektakel zum 25. Geburtstag von Motown im Civic Center von Los Angeles tritt Jackson sowohl solo als auch mit seinen Brüdern auf. Als die Show unter dem Titel „Motown 25: Yesterday, Today, Forever" im Fernsehen ausgestrahlt wird, werden Jacksons bahnbrechende Choreografie, sein Wippen mit den Zehen und seine Hutwürfe zu einem Schlüsselmoment der amerikanischen Popkultur. Im September wird die Show mit einem Emmy als „Herausragendes Varieté-, Musik- oder Comedy-Programm" ausgezeichnet.

Jackson se produit seul et avec ses frères pour les 25 ans de la Motown, lors du concert spectaculaire organisé au Civic Center de Los Angeles. Lorsque la soirée est diffusée à la télévision sous le titre «Motown 25: Yesterday, Today, Forever», la gestuelle et les pas de danse de Jackson, ses sursauts sur les pointes de pied et son toucher de chapeau entrent dans la légende. En septembre, cette retransmission reçoit l'Emmy Award du Meilleur programme de variété, de musique ou de divertissement.

SATURDAY, APRIL 30, 1983

Having already topped the British chart the previous week, Jackson hits No. 1 in the United States with *Beat It*, failing to replace himself at the top spot by only one week, the shortest gap registered since the Beatles' achievement in 1964. The self-penned smash is highlighted by searing guitar work by Eddie Van Halen—a genre-mixing idea conceived by producer Jones, which Van Halen agreed to do as a favor without being paid. Another hot video for the cut—directed by Bob Giraldi and costing $160,000—featuring two rival gangs who perform perfectly-timed synchronized dance steps, led and choreographed by Jackson with assistant choreographer Michael Peters—keeps the song in heavy rotation on MTV. Another groundbreaking video, its innovative dance sequences will be much copied over the next ten years.

Nachdem Jackson bereits in der Vorwoche an der Spitze der britischen Charts gelandet ist, erreicht er mit *Beat It* auch in den USA die Top-Position. Damit liegt nur eine Woche zwischen diesem und seinem vorigen Nummer-eins-Hit – die kürzeste Lücke seit den Beatles

1964. Ein Höhepunkt des selbst verfassten Hits ist Eddie Van Halens mitreißendes Spiel auf der E-Gitarre, ein Genre-Mix, den sich Produzent Jones ausgedacht hat und den Van Halen aus Gefälligkeit und ohne Gage lieferte. Ein weiteres heißes Video für diese Single sorgt dafür, dass die Nummer an führender Position in der MTV-Rotation bleibt. Es wurde für 160.000 Dollar unter der Regie von Bob Giraldi produziert und zeigt zwei rivalisierende Banden in einem perfekt abgestimmten Tanz, angeführt und choreografiert von Jackson mit Unterstützung seines Assistenten Michael Peters.

Déjà en tête des ventes britanniques depuis une semaine, Jackson atteint également la première place aux États-Unis avec *Beat It* . C'est la première fois qu'un artiste enregistre un écart si court (une semaine) entre deux places de numéro un depuis les Beatles, en 1964. Ce nouveau tube, qu'il a composé seul, brille par l'intervention à la guitare d'Eddie Van Halen – l'idée de ce mélange de genres revient à Quincy Jones, et Van Halen accepte de jouer le jeu. Là encore, le clip, réalisé par Bob Gilardi pour un budget de 160 000 dollars, marque les esprits : deux gangs rivaux s'affrontent dans une chorégraphie parfaitement orchestrée conçue par Jackson avec l'aide de Michael Peters, et cette fois MTV le diffuse en boucle. Le style et les pas de danse de ce clip seront souvent copiés.

"I want you to know that when I first agreed to tour, I decided to donate all the money I make from our performances to charity."

„Ihr sollt wissen, dass ich ... beschlossen hatte, alle meine Einnahmen aus unseren Auftritten für wohltätige Zwecke zu spenden."

« Lorsque j'ai accepté de participer à la tournée, j'ai décidé de faire don de tout l'argent que je gagnerai à des œuvres de charité. »

MICHAEL JACKSON, JULY 5, 1984

WEDNESDAY, NOVEMBER 30, 1983

The Jacksons announce plans for a major tour in 1984 at a press conference, with boxing promoter Don King offering $3 million in upfront advances. On the eve of the "Victory" tour in July, Michael will refute claims of greed (with regard to the exorbitant ticket prices), and announces that his entire earnings for the tour will go to charity. Three charities will benefit: The United Negro College Fund-established Michael Jackson Scholarship Fund, Camp Good Times for terminally ill children and the T. J. Martell Foundation for Leukemia and Cancer Research. He will also receive death threats during the tour.

Auf einer Pressekonferenz verkünden die Jacksons ihre Pläne für eine große Tour im nächsten Jahr, für die ihnen Boxpromoter Don King einen Vorschuss von drei Millionen Dollar geboten hat. Kurz vor Beginn der „Victory"-Tour im Juli wehrt sich Michael gegen Vorwürfe der Geldgier (aufgrund der exorbitanten Eintrittspreise) und gibt bekannt, dass er seinen gesamten Gewinn aus der Tour wohltätigen Zwecken stiften werde. Die

Nutznießer sind drei Organisationen: der vom United Negro College Fund gegründete Michael Jackson Scholarship Fund, das Camp Good Times für unheilbar kranke Kinder und die T. J. Martell Foundation für Leukämie- und Krebsforschung. Während der Tournee erhält Michael auch Morddrohungen.

Lors d'une conférence de presse, les Jackson annoncent une tournée monstre pour l'année suivante, aux côtés du promoteur de boxe Don King, qui leur a offert une avance de trois millions de dollars. En juillet 1984, à la veille du lancement de la tournée « Victory », Michael, accusé de cupidité (à cause du prix exorbitant des billets), déclare qu'il reversera l'ensemble de son cachet à des œuvres de charité. Il sera investi dans trois fondations : le Michael Jackson Scholarship Fund, intégré au United Negro College Fund, le camp de vacances Camp Good Times pour les enfants malades en phase finale, et la Fondation T. J. Martell pour la recherche sur la leucémie et le cancer. Il recevra plusieurs menaces de mort pendant la tournée.

FRIDAY, DECEMBER 2, 1983

MTV airs the seminal full-length 14-minute "Thriller" video for the first time. (Jackson's disclaimer at the beginning of the film is added when church elders of the Encino Kingdom Hall threaten him with expulsion because of its subject matter.)

MTV zeigt erstmals das Video „Thriller" in seiner vollen Länge von 14 Minuten. (Jacksons Distanzierung vom Inhalt wird zu Beginn des Films gesendet, nachdem

ihm die Kirchenältesten der Kingdom Hall in Encino aufgrund der Thematik mit Ausschluss gedroht haben.)

MTV diffuse pour la première fois le clip « Thriller », dans l'intégralité de ses 14 minutes mythiques. (L'avertissement de Jackson qui figure au début de ce courtmétrage musical est ajouté quand les dirigeants de l'église d'Encino Kingdom Hall le menacent d'excommunication en raison du sujet traité.)

MONDAY, JANUARY 16, 1984

Jackson collects seven trophies at the 11th annual American Music Awards, held at the Shrine Auditorium in Los Angeles: Special Award of Merit, Favorite Male Artist, Pop/Rock, Favorite Single, Pop/Rock, Favorite Album, Pop/Rock, Favorite Video, Pop/Rock, Favorite Male Artist, Soul/R&B, and Favorite Video, Soul/R&B—an unprecedented achievement.

Jackson heimst bei der 11. Verleihung der American Music Awards im Shrine Auditorium in Los Angeles, Kalifornien, sieben Trophäen ein, in den Kategorien „Special Award of Merit", „Favorite Male Artist, Pop/Rock", „Favorite Single, Pop/Rock", „Favorite Album, Pop/Rock", „Favorite Video, Pop/Rock", „Favorite Male Artist, Soul/R&B" und „Favorite Video, Soul/R&B" – eine beispiellose Leistung.

Jackson remporte sept prix à la 11ᵉ cérémonie des American Music Awards, qui se tient au Shrine Auditorium de Los Angeles : Meilleur artiste masculin, Meilleur simple, Meilleur album et Meilleur clip dans la catégorie Pop/Rock, ainsi que Meilleur artiste masculin et Meilleur clip dans la catégorie Soul/R & B – un exploit sans précédent qui lui vaut aussi un prix spécial du Mérite.

FRIDAY, JANUARY 27, 1984

Jackson is hospitalized at the Cedars-Sinai Medical Center with "second-degree burns on his skull," following an accidental flare explosion on the set of the second day of filming a Pepsi-Cola commercial at the Shrine Auditorium. A spark ignites his hair on the sixth take of the Giraldi-directed ad and Marlon Brando's son Miko, working as a bodyguard for the Jacksons, is the first to douse the flames. Pepsi will pay the singed star $1.5 million in compensation, which he will donate to the Brotman Memorial Hospital in Culver City, California, where he is treated.

Jackson wird mit „Verbrennungen zweiten Grades an seinem Schädel" ins Cedars-Sinai Medical Center eingeliefert, nachdem ihm eine unbeabsichtigte Explosion am zweiten Tag der Dreharbeiten zu einem Pepsi-Cola-Werbespot unter Bob Giraldis Regie im Shrine Auditorium die Haare in Brand gesetzt hat. Marlon Brandos Sohn Miko, der als Leibwächter für die Jacksons arbeitete, löschte als Erster die Flammen. Pepsi zahlt dem Star 1,5 Millionen Dollar Schmerzensgeld, die er dem Brotman Memorial Hospital in Culver City, Kalifornien, spendet, wo er behandelt wird.

Jackson est hospitalisé au Centre médical Cedars-Sinai pour des «brûlures au second degré du cuir chevelu»; il a été blessé par une explosion accidentelle survenue le deuxième jour de tournage d'une publicité pour Pepsi-Cola. Une étincelle a mis le feu à ses cheveux lors de la sixième prise d'une séquence conçue par Giraldi et le fils de Marlon Brando, Miko, qui fait partie des gardes du corps employés par les Jackson, s'est précipité pour éteindre les flammes. Pepsi verse à la star blessée un dédommagement d'un million et demi de dollars, dont il fait don au Brotman Memorial Hospital de Culver City (Californie), où il a été soigné.

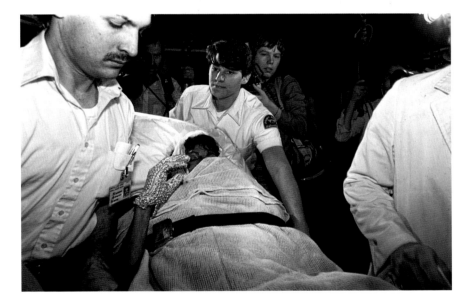

"I was pleased to learn that you were not seriously hurt in your recent accident. I know from experience that these things can happen on the set, no matter how much caution is exercised."

„Ich war erleichtert, als ich erfuhr, dass Sie bei Ihrem Unfall kürzlich nicht ernsthaft verletzt wurden. Aus Erfahrung weiß ich, dass solche Dinge am Set passieren können, wie viel Vorsicht man auch walten lässt."

« J'ai été heureux d'apprendre que votre récent accident ne vous a pas gravement blessé. Je sais d'expérience que ce genre de choses arrive sur un plateau, quelles que soient les précautions prises. »

PRESIDENT RONALD REAGAN, FEBRUARY 1, 1984

MONDAY, FEBRUARY 7, 1984
Jackson is inducted into **The Guinness Book of Records**, at the American Museum of Natural History in New York, as sales of *Thriller* shoot past 25 million.

Jackson wird im American Museum of Natural History in New York in das **Guinness-Buch der Rekorde** aufgenommen, als die Verkäufe von *Thriller* die 25-Millionen-Grenze überschreiten.

Jackson entre dans le **Livre Guinness des records**, au cours d'une cérémonie organisée au musée américain d'Histoire naturelle de New York : *Thriller* a dépassé les 25 millions d'exemplaires vendus.

"*Your deep faith in God and adherence to traditional values are an inspiration to all of us. You've gained quite a number of fans along the road since I Want You Back and Nancy and I are among them. Keep up the good work Michael. We're very happy for you.*"

„*Ihr tiefer Glaube an Gott und Ihr Festhalten an traditionellen Werten sind für uns alle eine Inspiration. Sie haben seit I Want You Back eine ganze Reihe von Fans gewonnen, und Nancy und ich gehören auch dazu. Machen Sie weiter so, Michael. Wir freuen uns für Sie.*"

«*Votre profonde croyance en Dieu et votre adhésion aux valeurs traditionnelles sont une inspiration pour nous tous. Vous avez conquis de nombreux fans depuis I Want You Back, et Nancy et moi en faisons partie. Continuez à faire du bon boulot, Michael. Nous sommes très heureux pour vous.*»

PRESIDENT RONALD REAGAN, FEBRUARY 7, 1984

TUESDAY, FEBRUARY 28, 1984

The day after the Pepsi-Cola commercial premieres on MTV and a week after he wins trophies for Best British Album (**Thriller**) and Best International Solo Artist at the third annual BRIT Awards in London, Jackson walks away with an unprecedented eight Grammys at the 26th annual ceremonies. The Gloved One's masterpiece **Thriller** wins eight awards, including Album of the Year and Best Engineered Recording (Non-Classical) for Bruce Swedien, while the extracted *Beat It* is named Record of the Year, and wins Jackson Best Rock Vocal Performance, Male. *Billie Jean* is named Best New Rhythm & Blues Song, as well as winning Jackson Best R&B Vocal Performance, Male, while *Thriller* is named Best Pop Vocal Performance, Male. Jackson and Quincy Jones are both hailed Producer of the Year. The Best Recording For Children category is also victorious for the Jackson-featured **E.T. The Extra-Terrestrial**.

Am Tag nach der Erstausstrahlung der Pepsi-Cola-Werbung auf MTV und eine Woche, nachdem er bei der 3. Verleihung der BRIT Awards die Auszeichnungen für das „Best British Album" (**Thriller**) und als „Best International Solo Artist" erhalten hat, werden Jackson bei der 26. Grammy-Verleihung acht Grammys verliehen. **Thriller** wird mit acht Preisen ausgezeichnet, unter anderem mit „Album of the Year" und „Best Engineered Recording (Non-Classical)" für Toningenieur Bruce Swedien, während die Auskopplung *Beat It* als „Record of the Year" gewürdigt wird und den Preis für die „Best Rock Vocal Performance, Male" erhält. *Billie Jean* wird zum „Best New Rhythm & Blues Song" gekürt und bringt Jackson wiederum die Auszeichnung als „Best R&B Vocal Performance, Male" ein. Für *Thriller* erhält er schließlich auch noch den Preis als „Best Pop Vocal Performance, Male". Jackson und Quincy Jones teilen sich die Auszeichnung als „Producer of the Year" sowie den Preis „Best Recording For Children" für das Album **E.T. The Extra-Terrestrial**.

Au lendemain de la première diffusion de la publicité pour Pepsi sur MTV et une semaine après avoir remporté à Londres les BRIT Awards de Meilleur album britannique (**Thriller**) et de Meilleur artiste international, Jackson repart de la 26ᵉ cérémonie des Grammys avec un record de huit trophées. **Thriller** est sacré Album de l'année et lui vaut le trophée de la Meilleure performance vocale masculine dans les catégories Rock (pour *Beat It*, également élu Titre de l'année), R & B (pour *Billie Jean*, nommé Meilleure chanson dans la catégorie New Rhythm & Blues) et Pop (*Thriller*). Bruce Swedien reçoit le prix du Meilleur arrangement (non-classique), tandis que Jackson et Quincy Jones reçoivent celui de Producteurs de l'année. Jackson rafle aussi un prix grâce à sa participation à **E.T. The Extra-Terrestrial**.

"Isn't this a thriller? I'm delighted to see all of you here. We haven't seen this many people since we left China. And just think, you all came to see me ... we have quite a few young folks in the White House who all wanted me to give you the same message. They said to tell Michael, 'Please give some TLC to the P.Y.T.s.' Now, I know that sounds a little off-the-wall, but you know what I mean."

„Ist das nicht ein echter Thriller? Ich freue mich sehr, Sie alle heute hier zu sehen. Wir haben nicht mehr so viele Menschen gesehen, seit wir aus China zurückgekommen sind. Und wenn man sich vorstellt, dass Sie alle gekommen sind, um mich zu sehen ... Es sind eine ganze Menge junger Leute im Weißen Haus, die alle wollten, dass ich Michael sage: ‚Bitte geben Sie den P.Y.T.s etwas TLC'. Ich weiß, das klingt ziemlich abgefahren, aber Sie wissen schon, was ich meine."

« Je suis très heureux de vous voir tous ici aujour-d'hui. Et à l'idée que vous êtes tous venus pour me voir... Il y a de nombreux jeunes gens à la Maison-Blanche, et ils m'ont tous demandé de vous faire passer un message. Ils m'ont dit : "S'il vous plaît, dites à Michael de donner du TLC (Tender Lovin' Care, tendresse, amour et réconfort) aux PYT (clin d'œil à la chanson Pretty Young Things)." Je sais que cela peut paraître un peu incongru, mais vous comprenez de quoi je parle. »

PRESIDENT RONALD REAGAN, MAY 14, 1984

MONDAY, MAY 14, 1984

During a visit to the White House to receive a Presidential Humanitarian Award from President and Mrs. Reagan, Jackson dons the jacket given to him by Hector Cormana, an elevator operator in New York.

Jackson erhält von Präsident Ronald Reagan und seiner Frau Nancy den „Presidential Humanitarian Award" für sein humanitäres Engagement. Jackson trägt dabei eine Jacke, die ihm der Fahrstuhlführer Hector Cormana aus New York geschenkt hat.

Au cours d'une visite à la Maison-Blanche, où il reçoit le Presidential Humanitarian Award des mains du président et de Mme Reagan, Jackson porte le blouson que lui a donné Hector Cormana, un conducteur d'élévateur new-yorkais.

SUNDAY, DECEMBER 9, 1984

After winning the Best Overall Performance Video, Best Choreography and Viewers Choice categories, all for "Thriller", at the inaugural MTV Video Music Awards in September and unveiling his Hollywood Star on the Walk of Fame last month, Jackson announces on the final night of the "Victory" tour at Dodger Stadium in Los Angeles, that it will be his last tour with his brothers, while singing Shake Your Body (Down To The Ground.) Over two million attended the 55 concerts, which grossed a record $75 million. Michael donates $5 million to the charities, as promised. Through their promotion of the tour, Pepsi-Cola achieve a larger market share than their rivals Coca-Cola for the first time.

Nachdem er für „Thriller" bereits die Auszeichnungen in den Kategorien „Best Overall Performance Video", „Best Choreography" und „Viewers Choice" erhalten und seinen Stern auf dem „Walk of Fame" in Hollywood enthüllt hat, verkündet Jackson im Dodger Stadium in Los Angeles beim letzten Konzert der „Victory"-Tour, während er Shake Your Body (Down To The Ground)

singt, dass dies die letzte Tour mit seinen Brüdern sei. Die 55 Konzerte spielten die Rekordsumme von 75 Millionen Dollar ein. Wie versprochen spendete Michael fünf Millionen Dollar für wohltätige Zwecke. Durch seine Werbepatenschaft für die Tournee erzielt Pepsi-Cola erstmals in seiner Geschichte einen größeren Marktanteil als der Konkurrent Coca-Cola.

« Thriller » a remporté les premiers MTV Video Music Awards du Meilleur clip, de la Meilleure chorégraphie et le prix du public en septembre, et Jackson a dévoilé son étoile sur le Walk of Fame de Hollywood en novembre. Au Dodger Stadium de Los Angeles, le dernier soir de la tournée «Victory», il annonce qu'il ne se produira plus avec ses frères alors qu'ils interprètent ensemble Shake Your Body (Down To The Ground). Plus de deux millions de personnes ont assisté aux 55 concerts de la tournée, qui a rapporté un record de 75 millions de dollars. Michael reverse 5 millions de dollars aux bonnes œuvres, comme il l'avait promis.

SUNDAY, MARCH 3, 1985

After "Making Michael Jackson's Thriller" is named Best Video Album at the 27th annual Grammy Awards the last week, Jackson visits the Madame Tussaud's Waxworks tourist attraction in London, which is inaugurating his waxwork lookalike. Traffic comes to a standstill on Baker Street, as Jackson jumps on to his car to wave to crowds. He also visits the legendary Abbey Road recording studios.

Nachdem „Making Michael Jackson's Thriller" bei der 27. Verleihung der Grammy Awards in der vergangenen Woche als „Best Video Album" ausgezeichnet wurde, besucht Jackson das Wachsfigurenkabinett Madame Tussaud's in London, wo sein Ebenbild aus Wachs vorgestellt wird. Der Verkehr auf der Baker Street kommt zum Erliegen, als Jackson auf sein Auto springt, um der Menge zuzuwinken. Er besucht auch die legendären Abbey-Road-Aufnahmestudios.

Alors que «Making Michael Jackson's Thriller» vient d'être élu Meilleur Album Vidéo de l'année lors de la 27ᵉ cérémonie des Grammy Awards, Jackson se rend au musée Madame Tussaud, à Londres, où est dévoilé le personnage de cire à son effigie. Le trafic s'immobilise sur Baker Street, lorsque Jackson grimpe sur sa voiture pour saluer la foule rassemblée. Il visite aussi les légendaires studios d'Abbey Road.

WEDNESDAY, AUGUST 14, 1985

Much to Paul McCartney's chagrin, Jackson, his friend and music collaborator, outbids the ex-Beatle in the acquisition of the ATV music publishing catalog, which includes a large portion of the Lennon and McCartney composition songbook, paying $47. 5 million for the company. Seen by McCartney as an act of betrayal, relationships with Jackson are permanently soured. (Jackson can afford it: he reportedly received a $58 million royalty check from Epic Records in May.)

Sehr zum Ärger von Paul McCartney überbietet ihn sein Freund und Kollege Michael Jackson beim Kauf der Rechte am ATV Music Publishing Catalog, der einen Großteil der von John Lennon und Paul McCartney komponierten Beatles-Songs enthält. Jackson zahlt dafür 47,5 Millionen Dollar. Paul McCartney betrachtet dies als Verrat, sein Verhältnis zu Jackson ist von nun an dauerhaft zerrüttet. (Jackson kann es sich leisten: Er hat im Mai angeblich 58 Millionen Dollar Tantiemen von Epic Records erhalten.)

Au grand regret de Paul McCartney, Jackson, son ami et partenaire musical, renchérit sur l'ex-Beatle et acquiert le catalogue musical d'ATV, qui comprend une grande partie des compositions de Lennon et McCartney, pour 47,5 millions de dollars. McCartney se sent trahi et les relations entre les deux hommes en seront à jamais gâchées. (Jackson peut se permettre cet achat : Epic Records lui aurait versé quelque 58 millions de dollars de droits d'auteur en mai.)

TUESDAY, FEBRUARY 25, 1986

We Are The World, the most successful single in American chart history to date, receives four awards at the 28th annual Grammys. The Jackson/Lionel Richie-penned song wins Record of the Year, Song of the Year, Best Group Pop Vocal Performance and Best Short Form Music Video. Producer Quincy Jones, in accepting the Record of the Year trophy, thanks "the generation that changed 'I, Me, My' to 'We, You, Us'." Recorded following last year's American Music Awards on January 28, 1985, *We Are The World* was written by Jackson and Richie in just two hours, following three days of preparation. After ten hours, only Richie and Jones remained, putting the final touches to an extraordinary recording which was released under the fundraising banner, USA For Africa.

We Are The World, bis heute die erfolgreichste Single der amerikanischen Chartgeschichte, erhält vier Preise bei der 28. Verleihung der Grammy Awards. Der von Michael Jackson und Lionel Richie geschriebene Song wird als „Record of the Year", „Song of the Year", „Best Group Pop Vocal Performance" und „Best Short Form Music Video" ausgezeichnet. Als er die „Record of the Year"-Trophäe entgegennimmt, dankt Produzent Quincy Jones „der Generation, die ‚ich, mir, mein' in ‚wir, dir, uns' umgewandelt hat". Die Aufnahme war im Anschluss an die Verleihung der American Music Awards des Vorjahres am 28. Januar 1985 entstanden. Jackson und Richie hatten *We Are The World* nach dreitägiger Vorbereitung in nur zwei Stunden zu Papier gebracht. Nach zehn Stunden im Studio blieben nur Richie und Jones, um einer außergewöhnlichen Aufnahme den letzten Schliff zu geben, die dann unter dem Wohltätigkeitsbanner „USA For Africa" auf den Markt kam.

We Are The World, le titre le plus populaire de l'histoire des ventes de disques américaines à ce jour, reçoit quatre trophées lors de la 28e cérémonie des Grammys. La chanson, écrite et composée par Jackson et Lionel Richie, repart avec les titres de Disque de l'année, Chanson de l'année, Meilleure performance vocale en groupe (catégorie Pop) et Meilleur clip musical court. Lorsqu'il accepte celui de Disque de l'année, le producteur Quincy Jones remercie «la génération qui nous a fait passer du "Je, moi, mon" au "Nous et vous, ensemble"». Le titre, composé en deux heures après trois petites heures de préparation, a été enregistré à l'issue des American Music Awards, le 28 janvier 1985. Au bout de dix heures de travail, Richie et Jones restent seuls en studio pour mettre la touche finale à cet enregistrement extraordinaire, commercialisé sous la bannière USA For Africa.

MONDAY, AUGUST 4, 1986

After Jackson's manager Frank DiLeo, business affairs adviser John Branca and PepsiCo president Roger Enrico complete Jackson's second contract for the soft drinks giant in May—this time for $15 million and including two further commercials and sponsorship of a solo world tour, Jackson and co-producer Jones move into Studio D at Westlake Studios to record a follow-up to *Thriller*. Jackson has already written 62 songs for consideration, and Jones invites outsiders to offer more. (The Beatles' *Come Together* is recorded, but rejected.) Jackson insists that his 300lb snake, Crusher, and constant chimp companion, Bubbles, are present at recording sessions. (Bubbles will enjoy studio rides on the back of engineer Bruce Swedien's Great Dane.)

Nachdem Jacksons Manager Frank DiLeo, sein Wirtschaftsberater John Branca und der Direktor von PepsiCo, Roger Enrico, im Mai Jacksons zweiten Vertrag für den Limonadenriesen ausgehandelt haben – diesmal über 15 Millionen Dollar, mit zwei weiteren Fernsehwerbespots und der Werbepatenschaft für eine Solo-Welttournee –, ziehen Jackson und Koproduzent Jones in das Studio D der Westlake Studios, um ein Nachfolgealbum für *Thriller* aufzunehmen. Jackson hat bereits 62 Songs geschrieben, und Jones bittet Außenstehende um weitere Vorschläge. (*Come Together* von den Beatles wird aufgenommen, aber abgelehnt.) Jackson besteht darauf, dass seine 136 Kilogramm schwere Schlange Crusher und sein ständiger Begleiter, der Schimpanse Bubbles, bei den Aufnahmen anwesend sind. (Bubbles genießt es, auf der Deutschen Dogge des Toningenieurs Bruce Swedien durchs Studio zu reiten.)

L'agent de Jackson, Frank DiLeo, le conseiller John Branca et Roger Enrico, le président de PepsiCo, ont signé un deuxième contrat en mai – cette fois pour 15 millions de dollars – en vertu duquel Jackson tournera deux nouvelles publicités pour le géant du soda, qui sponsorisera sa prochaine tournée mondiale solo. Jackson et Jones, coproducteur, entrent en studio à Westlake (ils travaillent dans le Studio D) pour enregistrer la suite de *Thriller.* Jackson a déjà écrit 62 chansons et Jones fait également appel à des contributions extérieures. (Ils enregistrent notamment une reprise de *Come Together*, des Beatles, qui ne figurera toutefois pas sur l'album.) Jackson insiste pour que son serpent de 150 kg, Crusher, et son chimpanzé, Bubbles, assistent aux séances d'enregistrement. (Bubbles prend grand plaisir à se rendre aux studios Westlake perché sur le dos du danois de Bruce Swedien.)

THURSDAY, SEPTEMBER 18, 1986

A year in the making, Jackson's 15-minute 3D space-fantasy film "Captain Eo," produced by sci-fi film-maker George Lucas, premieres at Disneyland in Anaheim, California, and the Epcot Center in Orlando, Florida. It includes the never-released dance number *We Are Just Here To Save The World*, written and performed by Jackson. During the time it took to make, exclusive distributor Disneyland/World built a movie theater on both sites specifically to accommodate the project.

Nach einjähriger Arbeit wird der fünfzehnminütige 3-D-Weltraum-Fantasy-Film „Captain Eo", produziert von Sci-fi-Filmemacher George Lucas in Disneyland im kalifornischen Anaheim und im Epcot Center von Walt Disney World in Orlando, Florida, uraufgeführt. Er enthält auch die nie zuvor veröffentlichte Dance-

Nummer *We Are Just Here To Save The World*, geschrieben und dargeboten von Michael Jackson. Während der Herstellung bauten Disneyland und Walt Disney World, die die exklusiven Vertriebsrechte besitzen, in beiden Parks je ein Kino eigens für dieses Projekt.

Après une année de travail, le court métrage de science-fiction en 3D de 15 minutes imaginé par Jackson et produit par le réalisateur George Lucas, « Captain Eo », est diffusé en avant-première au Disneyland d'Anaheim (Californie) et à l'Epcot Center d'Orlando (Floride). Jackson y chante notamment une composition inédite, *We Are Just Here To Save The World*. Le distributeur exclusif du film, Disneyland/Disneyworld profite du délai de fabrication pour faire construire sur les deux sites une salle de cinéma spéciale.

SUNDAY, SEPTEMBER 21, 1986

The **National Enquirer** magazine features on its front cover a picture of Jackson in what it purports to be an oxygen chamber, with the accompanying headline: "Michael Jackson's Bizarre Plan To Live To 150." (During a 1993 TV chat with Oprah Winfrey, Jackson will strongly refute this story, among many others which hint at his bizarre lifestyle, claiming that it was merely a picture of him lying in a burn victims' machine.)

Die Zeitung **National Enquirer** bringt auf ihrem Titelblatt ein Foto, das Jackson angeblich in einer Sauerstoffkammer zeigt, und dazu die Überschrift: „Michael Jacksons bizarrer Plan, 150 Jahre alt zu werden". (1993 wird Jackson diese und andere Geschichten über seine Lebensführung in einer Talkshow vehement dementieren und erklären, es habe sich um ein Foto gehandelt, das ihn in einer Maschine für Verbrennungsopfer zeige.)

Le magazine **National Enquirer** met en couverture une photo montrant Jackson dans ce qui est présenté comme un caisson à oxygène, accompagnée du gros titre suivant : « L'étrange projet de Michael Jackson : vivre jusqu'à 150 ans ». (Au cours d'un entretien télévisé de 1993 avec Oprah Winfrey, Jackson réfutera fermement cette histoire ainsi qu'une cohorte d'autres rumeurs sur ses bizarreries supposées, et affirmera que l'appareil en question est en fait une machine destinée aux personnes souffrant de brûlures.)

NOVEMBER 1986

Shooting takes place in New York on the video for the title cut from Jackson's forthcoming album, **Bad**. A 17-minute mini-film, directed by Martin Scorsese, its locations include the Bronx subway and the Dobbs Ferry School, and is based on the true story of Edmund Perry, a Harlem student who was shot by a plainclothes policeman, who claimed Perry had tried to mug him.

In New York wird das Video für den Titelsong von Jacksons nächstem Album **Bad** gedreht. Zu den Drehorten für die siebzehnminütige Filmsequenz unter der Regie von Martin Scorsese gehören die U-Bahn in der Bronx und die Dobbs Ferry School. Der Film basiert auf der wahren Geschichte von Edmund Perry, einem Schüler aus Harlem, der im Vorjahr von einem Polizisten in Zivil erschossen worden war, weil er diesen angeblich auf offener Straße habe ausrauben wollen.

Une fusillade éclate lors du tournage, à New York, du clip destiné au premier extrait du prochain album de Jackson, **Bad**. Le court métrage de 17 minutes, réalisé par Martin Scorsese, filmé notamment dans le métro du Bronx et à l'école Dobbs Ferry, s'inspire de l'histoire d'Edmund Perry, un étudiant de Harlem abattu par un policier en civil qui affirme que le jeune homme a tenté de l'agresser.

MONDAY, MAY 18, 1987

The Jehovah's Witnesses headquarters in Brooklyn, New York, issues a statement which says that the organization "no longer considers Michael Jackson to be one of Jehovah's Witnesses," by mutual agreement.

Das Hauptquartier der Zeugen Jehovas in Brooklyn, New York, erklärt öffentlich, dass die Organisation – in gegenseitigem Einvernehmen – „Michael Jackson nicht mehr als Zeugen Jehovas" betrachte.

Les Témoins de Jéhovah annoncent à Brooklyn que l'organisation « ne considère plus Michael Jackson comme un des Témoins de Jéhovah », décision prise d'un commun accord.

FRIDAY, MAY 29, 1987

Jackson allegedly offers $50,000 to buy the remains of the "Elephant Man," John Merrick. Although he eventually doubles his offer, it is rejected by the London Hospital. Despite denying the entire story during his 1993 "Oprah" interview, other sources subsequently claim that this original episode was leaked by Jackson's own publicity company.

Jackson bietet angeblich 50.000 Dollar für die sterblichen Überreste des „Elefantenmenschen" John Merrick. Obwohl er sein Angebot letztlich verdoppelt, lehnt das London Hospital ab. Wenngleich er die ganze Geschichte bei seinem Auftritt in der Talkshow „Oprah" 1993 abstreitet, behaupten andere Quellen später, Jacksons eigene Werbeagentur habe die Geschichte lanciert.

D'après la rumeur, Jackson aurait offert 50 000 dollars pour acquérir la dépouille de John Merrick, « Elephant Man ». Il aurait même doublé son offre, refusée par le London Hospital. Bien qu'il ait nié cette affaire au cours de son entretien avec Oprah, en 1993, d'autres sources ont ensuite affirmé qu'elle avait en fait été rendue publique par les publicitaires de Jackson.

MONDAY, JULY 13, 1987

50 of America's biggest record retail heads are invited to Jackson's Encino home to preview *Bad*. Hosted mainly by LaToya and Joe Jackson, dinner and a tour of the mansion are included, with the notoriously shy Michael appearing only briefly to pose for photos.

Fünfzig führende Vertreter des amerikanischen Schallplattenhandels werden zu einem Preview von *Bad* in Jacksons Haus in Encino eingeladen. Gastgeber sind Schwester LaToya und Vater Joe. Ein Abendessen und ein Rundgang durch die Villa sind inbegriffen. Der notorisch schüchterne Michael taucht nur kurz auf, um für ein paar Fotos zu posieren.

Les cinquante plus grands noms de l'industrie américaine de diffusion du disque sont invités dans la propriété de Jackson, à Encino, pour une présentation de *Bad* en avant-première. La soirée, orchestrée par LaToya et Joe Jackson, inclut un dîner et une visite de la maison et de ses dépendances. Michael, dont la timidité est de notoriété publique, ne fait qu'une brève apparition et pose pour quelques photos.

THURSDAY, AUGUST 27, 1987

Michael Jackson's *Bad* is previewed—four days ahead of release—on a Los Angeles radio station. The album has received the largest advance order in US history, with 2.2 million copies set to hit retail next week. On Monday, CBS will air the television special, "Michael Jackson—The Magic Returns," with the 17-minute video for *Bad* airing for the first time.

Michael Jacksons Album *Bad* wird vier Tage vor der Veröffentlichung von einem Rundfunksender in Los Angeles vorab gesendet. Für das Album liegen mehr Vorbestellungen vor als für jedes andere in der Geschichte der USA, und in der kommenden Woche werden 2,2 Millionen Exemplare an die Plattengeschäfte ausgeliefert. Am Montag strahlt CBS dazu die Sondersendung „Michael Jackson – The Magic Returns" im Fernsehen aus und zeigt dabei auch zum ersten Mal das siebzehnminütige Video zu *Bad*.

L'album *Bad* est diffusé en avant-première - quatre jours avant sa sortie - par une radio de Los Angeles. Il fait l'objet des plus importantes commandes de l'histoire américaine: les marchands de disques demandent pas moins de 2,2 millions d'exemplaires pour la sortie de l'album, la semaine suivante. Le lundi, CBS programme une soirée thématique intitulée « Michael Jackson — le retour de la magie » au cours de laquelle le clip de 17 minutes de *Bad* est diffusé pour la première fois.

SATURDAY, SEPTEMBER 12, 1987

With *Bad* debuting at No. 1 in Britain this week (repeating the feat in the United States in two weeks time,) Jackson begins his first solo tour with the first of 14 sellout dates at the Korakuen Stadium in Yokohama, Japan in front of 45,000 fans. He will break a world record, when 504,000 people attending seven shows, see him at Wembley Stadium in Wembley, London. The 123rd and final show will take place at the Los Angeles Memorial Coliseum & Sports Arena on January 24, 1989. 4.4 million people will attend the tour, which will gross over $125 million—the most ever by an entertainer. Jackson's personal entourage will be more than 250-strong, including a chef, hairdresser and manager DiLeo, who will handle all interviews. Also on the trip are his two current business managers, Jimmy Osmond (ex-Osmonds) and Miko Brando (son of Marlon).

Bad steigt in dieser Woche auf Platz eins in den britischen Charts ein (und schafft zwei Wochen später die gleiche Position in den USA), und Jackson beginnt im Korakuen-Stadion in Yokohama vor 45.000 Fans seine erste Solotournee mit einem von vierzehn ausverkauften Konzerten. Mit 504.000 Besuchern bei sieben Auftritten im Londoner Wembley-Stadion stellt er einen neuen Weltrekord auf. Das 123. und letzte Konzert der Tour wird am 24. Januar 1989 in der Los Angeles Memorial Coliseum & Sports Arena stattfinden. Insgesamt werden 4,4 Millionen Menschen die Konzerte dieser Tour besuchen, die über 125 Millionen Dollar einspielt – die höchste Summe, die je ein einzelner Entertainer erzielt hat. Jacksons persönliches Gefolge umfasst über 250 Personen, darunter ein Koch, ein Friseur und Manager DiLeo, der sämtliche Interviews gibt. Ebenfalls dabei sind seine beiden Geschäftsführer, Jimmy Osmond (der jüngste der singenden Osmond-Geschwister) und Miko Brando (Marlons Sohn).

Cette semaine-là, *Bad* entre directement à la première place du classement des meilleures ventes de disques britanniques, exploit qu'il réitère deux semaines plus tard aux États-Unis. Jackson entame sa première tournée solo par 14 concerts à guichet fermé au stade Korakuen de Yokohama (Japon), devant un public de 45 000 fans. Il bat le record du monde de fréquentation à Londres où 504 000 personnes assistent aux sept concerts du stade de Wembley. Le 123ᵉ et dernier concert a lieu au Memorial Coliseum & Sports Arena de Los Angeles le 24 janvier 1989. La tournée, qui attire 4,4 millions de fans en tout, rapporte plus de 125 millions de dollars - un nouveau record. L'entourage personnel de Jackson rassemble quelque 250 personnes, notamment un cuisinier, un coiffeur et son agent, DiLeo, qui répond à toutes les interviews. Ses deux managers du moment, Jimmy Osmond et Miko Brando (le fils de Marlon), font également partie du voyage.

TUESDAY, FEBRUARY 23, 1988

Following wins for Favorite Single, Soul/R&B category at the 15th annual American Music Awards and Best International Solo Artist award at the seventh annual BRIT Awards in London, Jackson begins on the North American leg of his "Bad" concert tour at the Kemper Arena in Kansas City, Missouri.

Nachdem er bei der 15. Verleihung der American Music Awards den Preis für die „Favorite Single, Soul/R&B" und bei der 7. Verleihung der BRIT Awards in London die Auszeichnung als „Best International Solo Artist" gewonnen hat, beginnt Jackson den nordamerikanischen Abschnitt seiner „Bad"-Konzerttournee in der Kemper Arena in Kansas City, Missouri.

Après avoir remporté les prix de Meilleur single dans la catégorie Soul/R & B aux 15ᵉ American Music Awards et le BRIT Award de Meilleur artiste international à Londres, Jackson entame la partie nord-américaine de sa tournée « Bad » à Kansas City (Missouri).

WEDNESDAY, MARCH 2, 1988

After he has performed *The Way You Make Me Feel* and *Man In The Mirror* at the 30th annual Grammy Awards held at New York's Radio City Music Hall, Jackson—nominated four times for **Bad**—comes away empty-handed—causing the **Los Angeles Times** to write that he "couldn't have looked any more heartbroken if someone had just run away with his pet chimp." He donates the box-office receipts of $600,000 from his Madison Square Garden concert to the United Negro College Fund.

Nachdem Jackson bei der 30. Grammy-Verleihung in der New Yorker Radio City Music Hall *The Way You Make Me Feel* und *Man In The Mirror* zur Aufführung gebracht hat, geht er trotz seiner vier Nominierungen für **Bad** am Ende leer aus, woraufhin die **Los Angeles Times** schreibt, er hätte „nicht niedergeschmetterter aussehen können, wenn jemand gerade mit seinem zahmen Schimpansen durchgebrannt wäre." Er spendet die 600.000 Dollar Einnahmen aus seinem Konzert im Madison Square Garden dem United Negro College Fund.

Après avoir interprété *The Way You Make Me Feel* et *Man In The Mirror* à la 30ᵉ cérémonie des Grammy Awards au Radio City Music Hall de New York, Jackson - nominé quatre fois pour **Bad** - repart les mains vides. Le **Los Angeles Times** écrit qu'il « semble bouleversé comme si on venait de kidnapper son chimpanzé apprivoisé. » Il fait don des 600 000 dollars de recettes que lui a rapportés son concert du Madison Square Garden à l'United Negro College Fund.

SATURDAY, MARCH 19, 1988

Jackson pays a reported $28 million for the Sycamore Ranch in Santa Ynez Valley, California, where he will live in grand style, creating his Neverland Ranch which includes his own zoo and theme park. At the end of the month, he will win a further two awards—Best Single, Male and Album of the Year, Male—at the second annual Soul Train Music Awards, held at the Civic Center in Santa Monica.

Jackson zahlt angeblich 28 Millionen Dollar für die Sycamore-Ranch im kalifornischen Santa Ynez Valley, wo er auf großem Fuß leben und seine Neverland-Ranch mitsamt eigenem Zoo und Vergnügungspark aufbauen wird. Am Monatsende erhält er bei der zweiten Verleihung der Soul Train Music Awards, die im Civic Center in Santa Monica, Kalifornien, stattfindet, zwei weitere Auszeichnungen – für die „Best Single, Male" und das „Album of the Year, Male".

Jackson débourse, selon la rumeur, 28 millions de dollars pour la propriété de Sycamore Ranch, dans la vallée de Santa Ynez (Californie), où il vit dans un luxe dispendieux : il y crée le ranch de Neverland, qui abrite notamment un zoo personnel et un parc d'attractions. À la fin du mois, il remporte deux nouveaux trophées – Meilleur titre et Meilleur album/interprète masculin – lors de la deuxième édition des Soul Train Music Awards, qui se tient au Civic Center de Santa Monica.

SUNDAY, MAY 15, 1988

With press silence still maintained, Jackson's autobiography, **Moonwalk**, debuts at No. 1 on the **New York Times** best-seller list. An immediate global best-seller, the book divulges that the millionaire regards himself as one of the loneliest people in the world.

Während Jackson der Presse gegenüber weiterhin schweigt, erscheint seine Autobiografie **Moonwalk** und klettert sofort auf Platz eins der Bestsellerliste in der **New York Times**. Das Buch, das weltweit zum Bestseller wird, enthüllt, dass sich der Millionär selbst als einen der einsamsten Menschen bezeichnet.

L'autobiographie de Michael Jackson, **Moonwalk**, sort en librairie : elle atteint immédiatement la première place de la liste des meilleures ventes de livres établie par le **New York Times.** Ce best-seller mondial révèle notamment que le milliardaire se considère comme une des personnes les plus seules au monde.

SATURDAY, JULY 16, 1988

In the midst of a record seven sellout dates at the Wembley Stadium in Wembley, seen by a total of 504,000 fans, Jackson presents audience members H. R. H. the Prince and Princess of Wales with a six-figure cheque for the Prince's Trust Charity. Bubbles is refused entry to England under strict quarantine laws, but tour companion, American television actor Jimmy Safechuck, is allowed in. He has appeared with Jackson in a recent Pepsi commercial and will also perform on stage. During the trip, Jackson visits venerable London toy store, Hamleys (where he buys a doll of himself), and record store HMV, when both agree to open for him after hours.

Bei einem von sieben ausverkauften Konzerten im Londoner Wembley-Stadion, die von insgesamt 504.000 Fans besucht werden, überreicht Jackson den Königlichen Hoheiten, dem Prince und der Princess of Wales, einen Scheck über einen sechsstelligen Betrag für den Prince's Trust Charity. Bubbles wird die Einreise in das Vereinigte Königreich aufgrund der strengen Quarantänebestimmungen zwar verweigert, aber der amerikanische Fernsehschauspieler Jimmy Safechuck, der Jackson ebenfalls auf seiner Tournee begleitet, darf einreisen. Während der Reise besucht Jackson den Londoner Spielzeugladen Hamleys (wo er eine Michael-Jackson-Puppe kauft) und den Plattenladen HMV, nachdem beide bereit waren, speziell für ihn nach Ladenschluss noch einmal zu öffnen.

Au cours des sept concerts à guichet fermé du Stade de Wembley à Londres (qui rassembleront au total 504 000 fans), Jackson remet au prince et à la princesse de Galles, présents dans le public, un chèque à six chiffres destiné à la fondation de Charles, la Trust Charity. Bubbles se voit refuser l'entrée sur le territoire britannique en vertu des lois de quarantaine. Pendant son séjour londonien, Jackson visite le célèbre magasin de jouets Hamleys (où il s'achète une poupée) et le magasin de disques HMV, qui acceptent tous deux de lui ouvrir leurs portes après l'heure de fermeture.

WEDNESDAY, SEPTEMBER 7, 1988

Jackson collects the prestigious Video Vanguard trophy at the fifth annual MTV Video Music Awards, held at the Universal Amphitheatre in Universal City, California—an honor subsequently named the Michael Jackson Video Vanguard Award.

Jackson erhält bei der 5. Verleihung der MTV Video Music Awards im Universal Amphitheatre im kalifornischen Universal City die angesehene Video-Vanguard-Trophäe, die ihm zu Ehren fortan den Namen Michael Jackson Video Vanguard Award trägt.

Jackson remporte le prestigieux prix Video Vanguard à la cinquième cérémonie des MTV Video Music Awards, qui se tient dans l'amphithéâtre Universal, à Universal City (Californie) – un trophée qui sera ensuite rebaptisé en son honneur le Michael Jackson Video Vanguard Award.

SUNDAY, OCTOBER 23, 1988

Jackson tours the house on West Grand Blvd., where Berry Gordy Jr. launched Motown Records in 1959. Jackson donates $125,000, a stage uniform from 1972, a rhinestone-studded glove and a hat to the Motown Museum, as he prepares for his sellout concerts on Tuesday and Wednesday at the nearby Palace of Auburn Hills.

Jackson besichtigt das Haus am West Grand Boulevard in Detroit, in dem Berry Gordy Jr. 1959 Motown Records aus der Taufe gehoben hatte. Jackson spendet dem Motown-Museum 125.000 Dollar, ein Bühnenkostüm aus dem Jahr 1972, einen strassbesetzten Handschuh und einen Hut, während er sich auf seine ausverkauften Konzerte am Dienstag und Mittwoch im Palace im benachbarten Auburn Hills vorbereitet.

En pleine préparation pour ses deux concerts au Palace d'Auburn Hills, Jackson visite la maison de West Grand Boulevard, toute proche, où Berry Gordy Jr. a lancé la Motown Records en 1959. Jackson fait don de 125 000 dollars, d'un costume de scène de 1972, d'un gant serti de strass et d'un chapeau au Motown Museum.

"I'm very happy and proud to be back to the soil from which I came. Berry Gordy is the man that made it all possible for me. I want to say thank you, Berry, and I love you."

„Ich bin sehr glücklich und stolz, wieder auf heimatlichem Boden zu stehen. Berry Gordy ist der Mann, der mir den Weg geebnet hat. Ich möchte dir danken, Berry, und ich liebe dich."

«Je suis très heureux et fier de revenir sur la terre qui m'a vu naître. Berry Gordy est l'homme qui m'a tout rendu possible. Je veux te dire merci, Berry, et je t'aime.»

MICHAEL JACKSON, OCTOBER 23, 1988

MONDAY, JANUARY 16 TO WEDNESDAY, JANUARY 18, THURSDAY, JANUARY 26 & FRIDAY, JANUARY 27, 1989

The "Bad" tour comes to a close with five sellout dates at the Los Angeles Memorial Coliseum & Sports Arena. At the final performance of the 123rd show tour, Jackson donates a portion of the proceeds to the Childhelp charity and dedicates a Motown medley to his former boss, Berry Gordy.

Die „Bad"-Tour endet mit fünf ausverkauften Konzerten in der Los Angeles Memorial Coliseum & Sports Arena. Bei der letzten Vorstellung der 123 Auftritte umfassenden Tour stiftet Jackson einen Teil der Einnahmen der Wohltätigkeitsorganisation Childhelp und widmet Berry Gordy ein Motown-Medley.

La tournée «Bad» s'achève par cinq concerts affichant complet au Memorial Coliseum & Sports Arena de Los Angeles. Lors du 123ᵉ et dernier concert de la tournée, Jackson fait don d'une partie des recettes à l'association Childhelp et dédie un medley de son répertoire Motown à son ancien mentor, Berry Gordy.

64

MONDAY, FEBRUARY 13, 1989

Presented with the Special Award of Achievement by Eddie Murphy at the 16th annual American Music Awards two weeks ago, Jackson now fires manager DiLeo, who reportedly seeks a $60-million settlement. Jackson also wins Best Music Video for "Smooth Criminal", Best International Solo Artist and Best International Artist, Male at the eighth annual BRIT Awards.

Nachdem ihm bei der 16. Verleihung der American Music Awards zwei Wochen zuvor der Sonderpreis überreicht wurde, feuert Jackson seinen Manager DiLeo, der angeblich eine Abfindung von 60 Millionen Dollar zu erpressen versucht. Jackson gewinnt bei der 8. Verleihung der BRIT Awards zudem die Preise „Best Music Video" für „Smooth Criminal", „Best International Solo Artist" und „Best International Artist, Male".

Deux semaines après avoir reçu des mains d'Eddie Murphy un American Music Award saluant l'ensemble de sa carrière, Jackson renvoie son agent, DiLeo, qui aurait cherché à lui soutirer 60 millions de dollars. Il remporte aussi les BRIT Awards de Meilleur clip pour «Smooth Criminal», et de Meilleur artiste international.

TUESDAY, MAY 2, 1989

Adding to his slew of awards at last month's third annual Soul Train Music Awards (Best R&B/Urban Contemporary Single, Male and Best R&B/Urban

Contemporary Music Video), Jackson, wearing a wig, fake mustache and false teeth, enters Zales jewellers in Simi Valley, California. Security guard H. N. Edwards, thinking him to be a robber, alerts police, who make Jackson strip off his disguise.

Nachdem er im vergangenen Monat bei der 3. Verleihung der Soul Train Music Awards zwei weitere Auszeichnungen erhalten hat („Best R&B/Urban Contemporary Single, Male" und „Best R&B/Urban Contemporary Music Video"), besucht Jackson mit Perücke, falschem Schnurrbart und falschem Gebiss den Juwelierladen Zales in Simi Valley, Kalifornien. H. N. Edwards, ein Sicherheitsbediensteter des Einkaufszentrums, hält ihn für einen Räuber und alarmiert die Polizei, die Jackson zwingt, seine Verkleidung abzulegen.

La collection déjà impressionnante de trophées décrochés par Jackson s'est encore agrandie le mois précédent, lors de la 3ᵉ cérémonie des Soul Train Music Awards (Meilleur single d'un artiste masculin et Meilleur clip dans la catégorie R & B/Urban Contemporary). Ce jour-là, Jackson met une perruque, une fausse moustache et un dentier pour se rendre chez le joaillier Zales, dans la Simi Valley (Californie). Un des vigiles du centre commercial le prenant pour un malfrat, alerte la police. Les trois voitures de patrouille découvrent avec surprise l'identité réelle de ce personnage suspect.

*"This is the happiest day of my life.
I love you all."*

*„Dies ist der glücklichste Tag meines Lebens.
Ich liebe euch alle."*

*« C'est le plus beau jour de ma vie.
Je vous aime tous. »*

MICHAEL JACKSON, OCTOBER 11, 1989

WEDNESDAY, SEPTEMBER 13, 1989
Jackson signs a $28-million deal with L. A. Gear Sportswear to be its spokesperson. The campaign will be unsuccessful and will be dropped after one commercial. During the month, a California Raisins commercial featuring a "claymation" version of Jackson airs on American TV. He donates his $25,000 royalty to charity.

Jackson schließt einen 28-Millionen-Dollar-Vertrag ab, der ihn verpflichtet, für den Sportartikelhersteller L. A. Gear zu werben. Die Kampagne floppt und wird nach nur einem Werbespot eingestellt. Im Laufe des Monats strahlen amerikanische Fernsehsender einen Werbespot für kalifornische Rosinen aus, in dem eine Jackson nachgebildete bewegte Knetfigur auftritt. Jackson spendet seine Tantiemen in Höhe von 25.000 Dollar für wohltätige Zwecke.

Jackson signe un contrat de publicité de 28 millions de dollars avec la marque L. A. Gear Sportswear, dont il devient un ambassadeur. La campagne fait un flop et est abandonnée après un seul spot. Une publicité pour les raisins secs de Californie avec un Jackson en pâte à modeler est diffusée à la télévision américaine. Il fait don de son cachet de 25 000 dollars aux bonnes œuvres.

WEDNESDAY, OCTOBER 11, 1989
Jackson attends a ceremony at his former Gardner Street Elementary School, where the Michael Jackson Auditorium is inaugurated. He has also pledged to pay the yearly salary of the school's music teacher.

Jackson wohnt einer Feier in seiner früheren Grundschule, der Gardner Street Elementary School, bei, wo ein Michael Jackson Auditorium eingeweiht wird. Er sagt zudem zu, für das Jahresgehalt des Musiklehrers der Schule aufzukommen.

Jackson assiste à une cérémonie organisée dans son ancienne école élémentaire, la Gardner Street Elementary School, pour l'inauguration de l'Auditorium Michael Jackson. Il s'engage également à payer le salaire annuel du professeur de musique de l'école.

THURSDAY, APRIL 5, 1990

Three weeks after he wins the Silver Award as the 1980s Artist of the Decade at the fourth annual Soul Train Music Awards, Jackson appears on the White House Lawn as the guest of President Bush, while in Washington to collect the Entertainer of the Decade Humanitarian Award from the Capitol's Children Museum. (Later in the month, he will attend the opening ceremonies for Donald Trump's Taj Mahal Hotel in Atlantic City, New Jersey.)

Drei Wochen nachdem er bei der 4. Verleihung der Soul Train Music Awards den Silver Award als „Artist of the Decade" der 1980er Jahre erhalten hat, taucht Jackson auf dem Rasen des Weißen Hauses als Gast von Präsident George Bush auf, während er Washington besucht, um vom Capitol's Children Museum den Preis „Entertainer of the Decade Humanitarian Award" entgegenzunehmen. (Im weiteren Verlauf des Monats wird er die Eröffnungsfeier für Donald Trumps Taj Mahal Hotel in Atlantic City, New Jersey, besuchen.)

Trois semaines après avoir empoché le Silver Award d'Artiste de la décennie 1980 lors des 4e Soul Train Music Awards, Jackson est invité à la Maison-Blanche par le président Bush. Il se trouve à Washington pour recevoir le Humanitarian Award d'Artiste de l'année décerné par le musée pour enfants du Capitole. (Plus tard ce mois-là, il assiste à l'inauguration de l'hôtel Taj Mahal de Donald Trump à Atlantic City).

"He does good work, what we call the 'Points of Light' concept. I just wanted to bring him out here and officially welcome him to the White House once again. Glad you're here, sir. Very pleased you're here."

„Er leistet gute Arbeit, was wir das „Points of Light"-Konzept nennen. Ich wollte ihn einfach hier zu uns rausbringen und ihn wieder offiziell im Weißen Haus willkommen heißen. Ich bin froh, dass Sie hier sind, Sir. Freut mich sehr, dass Sie hier sind."

« Il fait du bon travail, il œuvre pour ce que nous appelons les "points de lumière". Je voulais juste qu'il soit présent parmi nous aujourd'hui, et l'accueillir une fois encore officiellement à la Maison-Blanche. Content que vous soyez venu, monsieur. Très heureux que vous soyez là. »

PRESIDENT GEORGE BUSH

TUESDAY, MAY 8, 1990

To celebrate its 50th anniversary, the BMI presents its first Michael Jackson award to the singer himself at the Regent Beverly Wilshire Hotel, in Beverly Hills, California.

Zur Feier des 50. Jahrestags der Firmengründung überreicht BMI dem Sänger selbst seinen ersten Michael-Jackson-Preis im Regent Beverly Wilshire Hotel im kalifornischen Beverly Hills.

Pour célébrer ses 50 ans, le BMI remet le premier prix Michael Jackson au chanteur lui-même, lors d'une cérémonie organisée au Regent Beverly Wilshire Hotel de Beverly Hills.

SUNDAY, JUNE 3, 1990

Jackson is admitted to the St. John's Hospital & Health Center in Santa Monica, to undergo tests, after experiencing chest pains. He is diagnosed as having costochondritis, meaning that the cartilage at the front of his rib cage is inflamed. (Lawyer Thomas Wampold files a class-action lawsuit alleging Jackson was not sick, as he said, when he cancelled three Tacoma, Washington concerts, therefore committing a breach of contract and disappointing 72,000 fans.)

Jackson wird in das St. John's Hospital & Health Center in Santa Monica eingeliefert, um sich untersuchen zu lassen, nachdem er Schmerzen in der Brust verspürt hat. Es wird eine eine Kostochondritis diagnostiziert, d.h. eine Knorpelentzündung im Bereich des Brustkorbs. (Der Rechtsanwalt Thomas Wampold strengt eine Sammelklage gegen Jackson an, weil dieser nicht, wie behauptet, krank gewesen sei, als er drei Konzerte in Tacoma, Washington, abgesagt und damit seinen Vertrag gebrochen und damit seinen 72.000 Fans enttäuscht habe.)

Jackson est admis au St. John's Hospital & Health Center de Santa Monica pour subir des examens à la suite de douleurs thoraciques. Les médecins diagnostiquent une costochondrite, c'est-à-dire une inflammation des côtes et du cartilage situé à l'avant de la cage thoracique. L'avocat Thomas Wampold adresse un recours collectif contre Jackson en arguant que, contrairement à ce qu'il prétend, il n'était pas malade lorsqu'il a annulé trois concerts prévus à Tacoma (État de Washington), au grand désespoir des 72 000 spectateurs qui avaient payé leur place.

FRIDAY, SEPTEMBER 14, 1990

The Los Angeles Area Council of the Boys Scouts of America honors Jackson with the "Michael Jackson Good Scout Humanitarian Award", presented by Disney CEO Michael Eisner.

Der Lokalverband der amerikanischen Pfadfinderorganisation Boys Scouts of America für den Raum Los Angeles ehrt Jackson mit dem „Michael Jackson Good Scout Humanitarian Award", der ihm von dem Disney-Vorsitzenden Michael Eisner überreicht wird.

Le conseil des Boy Scouts d'Amérique du secteur de Los Angeles crée en l'honneur de Jackson une médaille spéciale, le « Michael Jackson Good Scout Humanitarian Award », que présente le PDG de Disney, Michael Eisner.

WEDNESDAY, MARCH 20, 1991

One week after his sister Janet has announced the most lucrative record deal in pop history, Jackson's new contract with Sony makes her agreement look inconsequential: with an $18-million cash advance for his forthcoming *Dangerous* album release alone, Jackson is made CEO of his own newly-formed Nation Records (which will change its name to to MJJ,) itself a subsidiary of the Jackson Entertainment Complex, which will also include TV, video and film divisions. His record royalty rate is negotiated at an unprecedented $2 and 8 cents per unit (album) with guarantees for post-*Dangerous* album advances of $5 million per project. Heralded as the first billion-dollar entertainer contract, it is also announced that movie directors David Lynch, Tim Burton, Christopher Columbus and Sir Richard Attenborough are already lined up to lense forthcoming promo film clips to accompany the *Dangerous* singles.

Nur eine Woche nachdem seine Schwester Janet den lukrativsten Plattenvertrag in der Geschichte der Popmusik bekannt gegeben hat, verblasst diese Nachricht angesichts des neuen Vertrags, den Michael mit Sony abschließt: Mit einem Vorschuss von 18 Millionen Dollar allein für sein Album *Dangerous* wird Jackson zum Direktor seines eigenen neu gegründeten Plattenlabels Nation Records, das eine Tochter des Jackson-Unterhaltungskonzerns ist. Seine Tantiemen betragen

beispiellose 2,08 Dollar pro Album, und für alle Alben nach *Dangerous* werden ihm Vorschüsse in Höhe von fünf Millionen Dollar je Projekt garantiert. Neben dem ersten „Milliarden-Dollar-Entertainer-Vertrag" wird außerdem bekannt gegeben, dass die Filmregisseure David Lynch, Tim Burton, Christopher Columbus und Sir Richard Attenborough bereits Schlange stünden, um Werbefilme für die Single-Auskopplungen aus dem *Dangerous*-Album zu drehen.

Une semaine après que sa sœur Janet a signé le contrat le plus lucratif de l'histoire de la musique pop, cette annonce est éclipsée par le nouveau contrat mirobolant conclu entre Jackson et Sony : la maison de disque lui verse en effet une avance immédiate de 18 millions de dollars pour son prochain album, *Dangerous*, et Jackson est nommé PDG d'un label spécialement créé pour lui, Nation Records (ensuite rebaptisé MJJ), qui fait partie du Jackson Entertainment Complex. Il négocie aussi une participation record de 2,80 dollars par album vendu, ainsi qu'une avance garantie de cinq millions de dollars pour chaque album produit après *Dangerous*. Lors de la présentation à la presse de ce contrat mirifique, le premier à neuf zéros décroché par un artiste seul, Sony annonce aussi que les réalisateurs David Lynch, Tim Burton, Christopher Columbus et Sir Richard Attenborough travailleront sur les clips de *Dangerous*.

MONDAY, MARCH 25, 1991

Jackson accompanies Madonna to the 63rd annual Academy Awards ceremony, held at the Shrine Auditorium.

Jackson begleitet Madonna zur 63. Verleihung der Academy Awards der Filmindustrie im Shrine Auditorium.

Jackson accompagne Madonna à la 63ᵉ cérémonie des Oscars, au Shrine Auditorium de Los Angeles.

THURSDAY, OCTOBER 3, 1991

The Detroit police recover Michael Jackson's crystal-beaded "Thriller" glove, stolen on Tuesday from the Motown Museum in Detroit. The item has been located in Grand Blanc, Michigan, where police arrest 23-year-old Bruce Hays from Flint, Michigan on a charge of larceny. MC Hammer had offered a $50,000 reward for its return, as part of a promotional gimmick for a dance-off challenge between the Hammer and the "King of Pop".

Die Polizei von Detroit findet Michael Jacksons strassbesetzten „Thriller"-Handschuh, der zwei Tage zuvor aus dem Motown Museum in Detroit entwendet worden ist. Man hat das Diebesgut in Grand Blanc, Michigan, entdeckt, wo die örtliche Polizei den dreiundzwanzig-jährigen Bruce Hays aus Flint, Michigan, wegen Diebstahls festgenommen hat. MC Hammer hatte eine Belohnung von 50.000 Dollar für die Wiederbeschaffung ausgesetzt als Teil eines Werbegags für ein Tanzduell zwischen Hammer und dem „King of Pop".

La police de Détroit retrouve le gant « thriller » brodé de perles en cristal (volé, le mardi précédent, au Musée Motown de la ville), à Grand Blanc (Michigan), où elle arrête Bruce Hays, 23 ans, habitant à Flint. MC Hammer avait offert une récompense de 50 000 dollars à la personne qui le rapporterait, dans le cadre d'un duel de danse entre Hammer et le « Roi de la Pop », organisé par leurs publicitaires respectifs.

THURSDAY, NOVEMBER 14, 1991

The video for *Black Or White*—the lead-off single from Jackson's long-awaited **Dangerous** album—premieres simultaneously on Fox, BET and MTV, and also BBC1-TV's "Top Of The Pops," which draws a 10.7 million audience for the show. The video will be withdrawn and re-edited after its first showing, amid controversy over its violent content. A week later, on the official release date of the new album, 30,000 copies, valued at $400,000, will be stolen from a terminal at Los Angeles Airport by three men brandishing shotguns.

Das Video für *Black Or White*, die erste Single-Auskopplung aus Jacksons lange erwartetem Album **Dangerous**, wird zeitgleich auf Fox, BET und MTV uraufgeführt und ebenso in der britischen Musiksendung „Top of the Pops", was der Show 10,7 Millionen Zuschauer beschert. Nach der Erstausstrahlung wird das Video aufgrund seiner umstrittenen Gewaltszenen zurückgezogen und umgeschnitten. Eine Woche später, am offiziellen Veröffentlichungstag des neuen Albums, werden 30.000 Alben mit einem Wiederverkaufswert von 400.000 Dollar von bewaffneten Räubern am Flughafen von Los Angeles gestohlen.

Le clip vidéo pour *Black Or White* – premier extrait très attendu de l'album **Dangerous** – est diffusé simultanément sur les chaînes américaines Fox, BET et MTV, ainsi que pendant l'émission «Top Of The Pops» de la BBC1-TV, regardée par 10,7 millions de téléspectateurs. Le clip sera remanié après cette première présentation, en raison de polémiques sur son contenu violent. Une semaine plus tard, le jour de sortie officiel du nouvel album, trois hommes armés en volent 30 000 exemplaires (valeur estimée : 400 000 dollars), à l'aéroport de Los Angeles.

MONDAY, FEBRUARY 3, 1992

Jackson holds a New York press conference from Radio City Music Hall to announce a forthcoming world tour to be sponsored by Pepsi, in the largest promotion deal ever. Proceeds will to go to his recently formed Heal The World foundation, devoted to helping children the world over. Video clip of the second cut from **Dangerous**, the jack-swing *Remember The Time*, featuring Eddie Murphy, model Iman (with whom Jackson shares his first screen kiss) and Earvin "Magic" Johnson in an Egyptian tale directed by John Singleton, premieres on multiple American cable channels at 8:25 p.m. EST.)

Jackson hält in der New Yorker Radio City Music Hall eine Pressekonferenz ab, auf der er seine bevorstehende Welttournee ankündigt, die im Rahmen des größten Werbedeals aller Zeiten von Pepsi gesponsert wird. Der Erlös wird an seine neu gegründete Stiftung Heal The World gehen, die Kindern in aller Welt helfen soll. Auf mehreren Kabelkanälen in den USA wird um 20:35 Uhr Ostküstenzeit der Videoclip zur zweiten Auskopplung aus **Dangerous**, *Remember The Time*, uraufgeführt, in dem der Komiker Eddie Murphy, das Model Iman (dem Jackson seinen ersten Leinwandkuss gibt) und der Basketballstar Earvin „Magic" Johnson unter der Regie von John Singleton ein ägyptisches Märchen nachspielen.

Jackson tient une conférence de presse au Radio City Music Hall de New York pour annoncer sa prochaine tournée mondiale, sponsorisée par Pepsi en vertu du plus gros contrat promotionnel jamais signé entre un artiste et une marque. Les recettes seront intégralement versées à la nouvelle fondation Heal The World créée par Jackson pour venir en aide aux enfants du monde. À 20 h 35 (heure de la côte est), les chaînes câblées américaines diffusent, pour la première fois, le clip réalisé par John Singleton pour le deuxième extrait de **Dangerous**, *Remember The Time*, un conte égyptien avec Eddie Murphy, le mannequin Iman (avec laquelle Jackson échange son premier baiser à l'écran) et Earvin « Magic » Johnson.

TUESDAY, FEBRUARY 11, 1992

Jackson begins a trip to Africa in Gabon, set to include visits to Tanzania and the Ivory Coast where Jackson will be crowned "King of the Sanwis" in the village of Krinjabo.

Jackson beginnt eine Afrikareise in Gabun und besucht unter anderem Tansania und die Côte d'Ivoire (die frühere Elfenbeinküste), wo er im Dorf Krinjabo zum „König der Sanwi" gekrönt wird.

Jackson entame au Gabon un voyage africain qui doit le mener en Tanzanie et en Côte d'Ivoire, où il doit être couronné « Roi des Sanwis » dans le village de Krinjabo.

"The only reason I am going on tour is to raise funds for the newly-formed Heal The World Foundation, an international children's charity, that I am spearheading to assist children and the ecology. My goal is to gross $100 million by Christmas 1993. I urge every corporation and individual who cares about this planet and the future of the children to help raise money for the charity. The Heal The World Foundation will contribute funds to pediatric AIDS in honor of my friend, Ryan White. I am looking forward to this tour because it will allow me to devote time to visiting children all around the world, as well as spread the message of global love, in the hope that others will be moved to do their share to help heal the world."

„Der einzige Grund, warum ich auf Tour gehe, ist der Wunsch, Gelder für die Stiftung Heal The World zu sammeln, um notleidende Kinder und den Umweltschutz zu unterstützen. Mein Ziel ist es, bis Weihnachten 1993 einen Erlös von 100 Millionen Dollar zu erzielen. Ich bitte alle Unternehmen und Privatpersonen mitzuhelfen, Geld für diesen guten Zweck aufzubringen. Die Stiftung Heal The World setzt sich zu Ehren meines Freundes Ryan White für die Behandlung von Aids bei Kindern ein. Ich freue mich auf diese Tour, weil ich mir die Zeit nehmen werde, Kinder in der ganzen Welt zu besuchen und die Botschaft von weltumspannender Liebe zu verkünden, in der Hoffnung, dass andere dazu bewegt werden, ihren Beitrag zur Heilung dieser Welt zu leisten."

« La seule raison qui me pousse à faire des tournées, c'est de lever des fonds pour la fondation Heal The World, qui vient en aide aux enfants et protège leur environnement. Mon but est de rassembler 100 millions de dollars d'ici Noël 1993. Je demande à toutes les entreprises et toutes les personnes d'aider les organisations humanitaires. Heal The World financera les traitements pédiatriques du sida, en hommage à mon ami Ryan White. Je suis impatient de commencer cette tournée parce qu'elle va me donner l'occasion de rendre visite à des enfants du monde entier, et de répandre un message d'amour universel, dans l'espoir d'émouvoir suffisamment les gens pour qu'eux aussi s'investissent dans la guérison du monde. »

MICHAEL JACKSON, FEBRUARY 1992

*"The American sacred beast took it upon himself to remind us we are underdeveloped and impure.
Our air is polluted, infested with germs. And it's not this mutant genius, this voluntary mutant,
this re-created being, bleached, neither white nor black, neither man nor woman,
so delicate, so frail, who will inhale it."*

*„Die heilige Kuh aus Amerika hat es auf sich genommen, uns in Erinnerung zu rufen, dass wir
unterentwickelte Schmutzfinken sind. Unsere Luft ist verdreckt und von Erregern verpestet.
Und dieses mutierende Genie, dieser vorsätzliche Mutant, dieses Wesen aus der Retorte, gebleicht,
weder weiß noch schwarz, weder Mann noch Frau, so empfindlich, so zart, ist nicht der Typ,
der sie einatmen wird."*

*«La vache sacrée américaine a pris soin de nous rappeler que nous étions impurs et
sous-développés. Notre air est pollué, infesté de microbes. Et ce n'est certainement pas ce génie
mutant, ce mutant volontaire, cet être re-créé, délavé, ni blanc ni noir, ni homme ni femme,
si délicat, si frêle, qui se risquerait à l'inhaler.»*

IVORY COAST NEWSPAPER ABIDJIAN, FEBRUARY 1992

WEDNESDAY, FEBRUARY 19, 1992
Jackson arrives at England's Stansted Airport, after
cutting short his African tour, amid stories that he is
concerned about his health. While in England with his
ten-year-old cousin Brett, he visits ailing British come-
dian Benny Hill, who is recovering from a heart attack.

Jackson landet auf dem Flughafen Stansted in England, nachdem er seine Afrikareise abgekürzt hat, weil er
Spekulationen zufolge um seine Gesundheit fürchtete.

Er trifft seinen zehnjährigen Cousin Brett in England und
besucht den kranken britischen Komiker Benny Hill.

Jackson arrive à l'aéroport anglais de Stansted
après avoir écourté son passage en Afrique. Selon la
rumeur, il aurait craint de mettre sa santé en danger.
Alors qu'il se trouve en Angleterre avec son cousin de
dix ans, Brett, il rend visite au célèbre comique britannique Benny Hill, qui se remet d'une crise cardiaque.

SATURDAY, JUNE 27, 1992

A multi-million dollar production, his "Dangerous" world tour opens in Munich, Germany, at the Olympic Stadium set to close in Mexico City, Mexico on November 11, 1993 (three months earlier than planned due to illness.) Sponsored by Pepsi-Cola, Jackson will perform to some 3,900,000 fans at 89 concerts on four continents. Two Boeing 747 jet aircraft are used to transport more than 100 tons of stage equipment to each city. (500,000 cassette copies of the single *Someone Put Your Hand Out*, previously unavailable anywhere, are released in Europe through a Pepsi deal, made possible by returning tokens printed on Pepsi packaging.)

Die mehrere Millionen Dollar teure „Dangerous"-Welttournee beginnt im Münchner Olympiastadion und wird am 11. November 1993 in Mexiko-Stadt vorzeitig beendet (wegen Erkrankung Jacksons). Unter der Werbepatenschaft von Pepsi wird Jackson insgesamt 89 Konzerte vor 3.900.000 Fans auf vier Erdteilen geben. Zwei Düsenflugzeuge des Typs Boeing 747 werden eingesetzt, um die mehr als hundert Tonnen Ausrüstung von Stadt zu Stadt zu befördern. (Eine halbe Million Kopien der Single *Someone Put Your Hand Out* auf Kassette, die zuvor nirgendwo erhältlich war, werden in Europa an Kunden verteilt, die Sammelpunkte von Pepsi-Verpackungen einsenden.)

La tournée «Dangerous», une machine de plusieurs millions de dollars, débute au Stade olympique de Munich et s'achèvera à Mexico le 11 novembre 1993 (trois mois plus tôt que prévu, en raison de problèmes de santé). Quelque 3 900 000 fans des quatre continents assistent aux 89 concerts de la tournée sponsorisée par Pepsi-Cola. Deux Boeing 747 sont utilisés pour transporter les 100 tonnes d'équipement et de décors d'une ville à l'autre. Pepsi lance dans le même temps une immense campagne promotionnelle. (500 000 cassettes du titre inédit *Someone Put Your Hand Out* sont distribuées aux consommateurs de la marque qui renvoient leurs coupons d'achat découpés sur les emballages.)

THURSDAY, JULY 30, 1992
& FRIDAY, JULY 31, 1992

The "Dangerous" tour arrives in England, with Jackson playing two sellout dates before 144,000 fans at Wembley Stadium. A third date is postponed when he succumbs to a viral infection. His arrival is not without controversy as he sues the **Daily Mirror** for libel and breach of contract, after it prints a less-than-flattering color photo of him on the front page. Meanwhile, the South African government has seen fit to ban his "In The Closet" video from TV broadcast, saying that it is "of a very sensual nature, which could offend viewers."

Die „Dangerous"-Tour erreicht England, wo Jackson zwei Konzerte vor 144.000 Fans im Wembley-Stadion gibt. Ein drittes Konzert wird verschoben, als er sich eine Virusinfektion zuzieht. Seine Ankunft verläuft nicht ohne Zwischenfälle: Jackson verklagt den **Daily Mirror** wegen Verleumdung und Vertragsbruchs, nachdem die Zeitung auf der Titelseite ein wenig

schmeichelhaftes Foto des Künstlers abgedruckt hat. In der Zwischenzeit sieht sich die Regierung Südafrikas genötigt, die Ausstrahlung seines Videos „In The Closet" zu verbieten, weil es „sehr sinnlicher Natur" sei und die Gefühle der Zuschauer verletzen könne.

La tournée « Dangerous » arrive en Angleterre : Jackson chante deux soirs à Wembley, devant 144 000 spectateurs. Une troisième date est annulée lorsqu'il est victime d'une infection virale. Son arrivée est teintée de scandale, puisqu'il attaque pour calomnie et rupture de contrat le **Daily Mirror**, qui a publié en couverture une photo couleur peu flatteuse de lui. Dans le même temps, le gouvernement sud-africain interdit la diffusion du clip « In The Closet », qu'il juge « d'une nature très sensuelle susceptible de heurter la sensibilité du public ».

WEDNESDAY, SEPTEMBER 2, 1992

Jackson's taped poem is broadcast on syndicated-TV's "Maury Povich Show" featuring AIDS victim Ryan White's mother Jeanne, who continues to campaign for AIDS education: "I miss you Ryan White, you showed us how to stand and fight, in the rain. You were a cloudburst of joy, the sparkle of hope in every girl and boy. Ryan White, I love you."

Ein von Jackson auf Band aufgezeichnetes Gedicht wird in der „Maury Povich Show" landesweit ausgestrahlt. Im Mittelpunkt der Sendung steht Jeanne White, deren Sohn Ryan 1990 an Aids gestorben ist und die sich für die Aids-Aufklärung einsetzt: „Ich vermisse dich, Ryan White, / du hast uns gezeigt, wie man steht

und kämpft, / im Regen. Du warst ein Lichtblick der Freude, / der Hoffnungsschimmer in jedem Mädchen und Jungen. / Ryan White, ich liebe dich."

L'émission indépendante «Maury Povich Show» est consacrée à la mémoire de Ryan White, victime du sida, et au combat de sa mère Jeanne pour davantage de prévention par l'éducation. La chaîne diffuse un poème enregistré par Jackson : «Tu me manques, Ryan White, tu nous as montré comment résister et combattre, sous la pluie. Tu as été une ondée de joie, l'étincelle d'espoir qui brille dans chaque fille et chaque garçon. Ryan White, je t'aime.»

WEDNESDAY, SEPTEMBER 9, 1992

During the European leg of his "Dangerous" tour, Jackson's performance of *Black Or White* is broadcast live via satellite from Wembley Stadium, to the ninth annual MTV Video Music Awards held at the Pauley Pavilion in Los Angeles.

Während der Europaetappe seiner „Dangerous"-Tour wird Jacksons *Black Or White* live über Satellit aus dem Wembley-Stadion zu der 9. Verleihung der MTV Video Music Awards in den Pauley-Pavillon in Los Angeles übertragen.

La 9ᵉ cérémonie des MTV Video Music Awards – qui se tient au Pauley Pavilion de Los Angeles – se connecte par satellite avec le stade de Wembley pour retransmettre en direct l'interprétation par Jackson de *Black Or White*, en pleine partie européenne de la tournée «Dangerous».

MONDAY, OCTOBER 5, 1992

Jackson visits a Harley Street doctor in London, concerned about his throat problems, before flying home to Los Angeles, canceling the last six dates of his European tour.

Jackson sucht einen Arzt in der Londoner Harley Street auf, weil er sich Sorgen wegen seiner Kehlkopf-probleme macht, bevor er die letzten sechs Konzerte seiner Europatournee absagt und zurück nach Los Angeles fliegt.

Jackson consulte un médecin exerçant sur Harley Street, à Londres, pour des problèmes persistants à la gorge ; il reprend l'avion pour Los Angeles, et fait annuler les six dernières dates de sa tournée européenne.

TUESDAY, NOVEMBER 24, 1992

Jackson's Heal The World Foundation airlifts medical supplies to war-torn Sarajevo—in conjunction with AmeriCares—from New York's JFK Airport. The cargo—valued at $2.1 million—includes medical supplies, clothing, shoes and blankets.

Jacksons Stiftung Heal The World fliegt zusammen mit AmeriCares Hilfsgüter vom New Yorker Flughafen JFK in die vom Krieg gezeichnete Stadt Sarajewo. Die Ladung im Wert von 2,1 Millionen Dollar umfasst medizinische Hilfsmittel, Kleidung, Schuhe und Decken.

La fondation Heal The World de Jackson affrète avec l'organisation caritative AmeriCares un avion à destination de Sarajevo, ravagée par la guerre. L'appareil décolle de l'aéroport JFK de New York avec à son bord un chargement estimé à 2,1 millions de dollars, composé de matériel médical, de vêtements, de chaussures et de couvertures.

SATURDAY, JANUARY 16, 1993

Jackson receives the Silver Anniversary Entertainer of the Year award and "Black Or White" wins the Music Video Award at the 25th annual NAACP Image Awards, held at the Civic Auditorium in Pasadena, California.

Zum Silberjubiläum der NAACP Image Awards im Civic Auditorium von Pasadena, Kalifornien, erhält Jackson bei der 25. Preisverleihung die Auszeichnung als „Entertainer of the Year", während „Black Or White" mit dem „Music Video Award" gewürdigt wird.

Jackson reçoit le prix Silver Anniversary d'Artiste de l'année et «Black Or White» remporte un Music Video Award à la 25ᵉ cérémonie des NAACP Image Awards au Civic Auditorium de Pasadena.

TUESDAY, JANUARY 19, 1993

Jackson performs Gone Too Soon, a tribute to Ryan White, and Heal The World at President-elect Bill Clinton's "An American Reunion—The 52nd Presidential Gala" inaugural concert from the Capital Centre in Landover, Maryland.

Im Rahmen des Amtseinführungskonzerts „An American Reunion - The 52nd Presidential Gala" des neu gewählten US Präsidenten Bill Clinton singt Jackson im Capital Centre in Landover, Maryland, Heal The World und Gone Too Soon, ein Tribut an Ryan White.

Jackson interprète Gone Too Soon (hommage à Ryan White) et Heal The World lors du gala inaugural de la présidence Clinton «An American Reunion: The 52nd Presidential Gala», au Capital Centre de Landover (Maryland).

MONDAY, JANUARY 25, 1993

In addition to opening the show with a performance of *Dangerous*, Jackson nabs the Favorite Album, Pop/Rock, and Favorite Single, Soul/R&B trophies at the 20th annual American Music Awards. He is also the recipient of the first-ever Michael Jackson International Artist Award, presented to him by longtime friend and confidant, Elizabeth Taylor.

Jackson eröffnet nicht nur die 20. Verleihung der American Music Awards mit einer Darbietung von *Dangerous*, sondern heimst auch gleich die Preise in den Kategorien „Favorite Album, Pop/Rock" und „Favorite Single, Soul/R&B" ein. Er erhält außerdem den allerersten „Michael Jackson International Artist Award" aus der Hand seiner langjährigen Freundin und Vertrauten Elizabeth Taylor.

Jackson ouvre la 20ᵉ cérémonie des American Music Awards avec *Dangerous*, et remporte les trophées de Meilleur album (Pop/Rock) et Meilleur single (Soul/ R & B), ainsi que le tout premier Michael Jackson International Artist Award, que lui remet son amie et confidente de longue date, Elizabeth Taylor.

SUNDAY, JANUARY 31, 1993

Jackson performs at half-time of "Superbowl XXVII," between the Dallas Cowboys and the Buffalo Bills, at the Rose Bowl in Pasadena. (The show will be seen by a record-setting estimated 133.4 million people, according to Nielsen Media Research.)

Jackson tritt in der Halbzeitshow des Super Bowl XXVII auf, bei dem die Dallas Cowboys in der Rose Bowl von Pasadena auf die Buffalo Bills treffen. (Dem Medienforschungsunternehmen Nielsen zufolge erzielt die Show mit 133,4 Millionen Zuschauern einen neuen Fernsehrekord.)

Jackson se produit au Rose Bowl de Pasadena endant la mi-temps du «Superbowl XXVII», qui oppose les Dallas Cowboys aux Buffalo Bills. (La retransmission du match est suivie d'un nombre record de téléspectateurs, estimé à 133,4 millions par l'institut de sondage Nielsen Media Research.)

WEDNESDAY, FEBRUARY 10, 1993

Jackson conducts his first TV interview in 14 years on a special edition of "Oprah Winfrey," broadcast live from his Neverland Ranch. During the candid conversation, Jackson admits to "cry(ing) through loneliness at age eight. I didn't have any friends growing up. I'd wash my face in the dark and my father would tease me. He was very strict." Concerning a list which Oprah details about persistent press rumors, Jackson claims that he didn't buy or want the Elephant Man bones (despite an original press release being issued by his own cohorts when the story first emerged.) On the subject of his much-changed skin color he states: "I have a skin disorder which destroys the pigment of my skin. It's in my family. We're trying to control it. I am a black American." Asked about his notorious crotch-grabbing he responds: "I'm slave to the rhythm." On his personal life Jackson says that he is dating Brooke Shields and that "I have been in love two times." When probed on the question of virginity, he quietly responds: "I'm a gentleman. Call me old-fashioned." At the interview's end, which has taken place in his house and while walking through his funfair and private cinema (in which he has erected beds in private booths so that terminally sick kids can watch films), he introduces the world premiere of *Give In To Me*, a concert video clip featuring Slash.

Jackson gibt sein erstes Fernsehinterview in 14 Jahren in einer Sonderausgabe der Talkshow „Oprah", die live von seiner Neverland Ranch übertragen wird. In diesem offenen Gespräch gesteht Jackson, dass er sich im Alter von acht Jahren „durch die Einsamkeit geweint" habe. „Ich hatte keine Freunde, als ich aufwuchs. Ich wusch mir im Dunkeln mein Gesicht, und mein Vater hänselte mich. Er war sehr streng." Auf eine Liste hartnäckiger Mediengerüchte, die ihm Oprah Winfrey vorliest, antwortet er, er habe (im Widerspruch zu einer Pressemitteilung aus seinen eigenen Reihen, als die Geschichte erstmals publik wurde) niemals die Knochen des „Elefantenmenschen" kaufen oder besitzen wollen. Zu seiner stark veränderten Hautfarbe erklärt er: „Ich leide unter einer Hautkrankheit, die die Pigmente meiner Haut zerstört. Es liegt in meiner Familie. Wir versuchen, es unter Kontrolle zu halten. Ich bin ein schwarzer Amerikaner." Auf die Frage, weshalb er sich ständig in den Schritt fasse, antwortet er: „Ich bin ein Sklave des Rhythmus." Zu seinem Privatleben meint Jackson, er gehe mit Brooke Shields aus und sei „zweimal verliebt gewesen". Auf die Frage nach seiner Jungfräulichkeit antwortet er ruhig: „Ich bin ein Ehrenmann. Nennen Sie mich altmodisch." Am Ende des Interviews, das in seinem Haus und während eines Spaziergangs über seinen Rummelplatz und durch sein Kino stattfindet (in dem er Betten für kranke Kinder aufgestellt hat), stellt er die Welturaufführung von

Give In To Me vor, einen Konzertvideoclip mit dem Gitarristen Slash.

Jackson répond à sa première interview télévisée depuis 14 ans pour une édition spéciale de l'émission «Oprah Winfrey», réalisée en direct de Neverland. Au cours de la conversation, Jackson avoue avoir «pleuré de solitude à l'âge de 8 ans. Je n'avais pas d'ami quand j'étais enfant. Je me lavais le visage dans le noir et mon père se moquait de moi. Il était très sévère.» Lorsque Oprah passe en revue les diverses rumeurs qui persistent dans la presse, Jackson répond point par point. Il affirme notamment ne pas avoir tenté d'acheter la dépouille d'Elephant Man (alors que son propre entourage a diffusé un communiqué de presse au moment des faits). Concernant le blanchissement progressif de sa peau, il déclare : «Je souffre d'une maladie qui détruit le pigment de la peau. C'est de famille. Nous essayons de la contrôler. Je suis un Noir américain.» À propos de sa célèbre habitude de saisir son entrejambe, il répond : «Je suis l'esclave du rythme.» Pour ce qui est de sa vie personnelle, Jackson déclare sortir avec Brooke Shields et être «tombé amoureux deux fois». Interrogé sur la virginité, il répond : «Je suis un gentleman. Vieux jeu, si vous préférez.» À la fin de l'entretien, qui s'est déroulé chez lui à la maison, puis au cours d'une promenade à travers sa fête foraine privée et une visite de sa salle de cinéma (dans laquelle il a fait installer des lits dans des cabines individuelles pour que les enfants malades en phase finale puissent aussi voir les films), il présente en avant-première mondiale *Give In To Me*, un clip de concert avec le guitariste Slash.

WEDNESDAY, FEBRUARY 24, 1993

As **Dangerous** continues its climb back up the United States chart (hitting No. 10 on March 6), following Jackson's current unexpected rush of participatory media promotion, he receives the Grammy Legend Award from his sister Janet at the 35th annual Grammy Awards, held at the Shrine Auditorium.

Während **Dangerous** im Kielwasser von Jacksons unerwarteter neuerlicher Medienpräsenz in den US-Charts wieder nach oben klettert (und am 6. März auf Platz zehn landet), erhält er bei der 35. Verleihung der Grammy Awards im Shrine Auditorium den „Grammy Legend Award" aus der Hand seiner Schwester Janet.

Alors que **Dangerous** continue son ascension dans le classement américain (il se place en 10ᵉ position le 6 mars) à la faveur de l'étonnante campagne de promotion à laquelle Jackson participe, il reçoit le Grammy Legend Award des mains de sa sœur Janet au Shrine Auditorium.

TUESDAY, MARCH 9, 1993

Jackson collects the Best R&B/Soul Album (*Dangerous*) and Best R&B/Soul Male Single (*Remember The Time*) trophies at the seventh annual Soul Train Music Awards, held at the Shrine Auditorium. He also performs *Remember The Time* in a wheelchair (the first time he has ever done this.)

Jackson gewinnt die Auszeichnungen in den Kategorien „Best R&B/Soul-Album" (*Dangerous*) und „Best R&B/Soul Male Single" (*Remember the Time*) bei der 7. Verleihung der Soul Train Music Awards im Shrine Auditorium. Zum ersten Mal singt er außerdem *Remember The Time* im Rollstuhl.

Jackson repart du Shrine Auditorium avec les Soul Train Music Awards de Meilleur album R & B/Soul (*Dangerous*) et Meilleur single R & B/Soul d'un artiste masculin (*Remember The Time*). Il interprète aussi *Remember The Time* assis dans un fauteuil roulant, pour la première fois.

FRIDAY, MARCH 12, 1993

The day after he attends the American Film Institute's dinner at the Beverly Hilton Hotel in Los Angeles, to bestow upon Elizabeth Taylor its Life Achievement Award, Jackson announces—by satellite—that he will be teaming up with former President Carter to help immunize thousands of pre-school children in Atlanta, as part of the Atlanta Project.

Einen Tag nachdem er einem feierlichen Abendessen des American Film Institute im Beverly Hilton Hotel in Los Angeles beigewohnt hat, um Elizabeth Taylor den Preis des AFI für ihr Lebenswerk zu überreichen, verkündet Jackson über Satellit, dass er den früheren US-Präsidenten Jimmy Carter unterstützen wolle, im Rahmen des Atlanta-Projekts Tausende von Vorschulkindern in Atlanta zu impfen.

Jackson, qui a assisté la veille au dîner de l'American Film Institute, au Beverly Hilton Hotel de Los Angeles, pour remettre à Elizabeth Taylor un Life Achievement Award, annonce – par liaison satellite – qu'il va s'associer à l'ancien président Carter pour aider à vacciner des milliers de jeunes enfants vivant à Atlanta, dans le cadre du Projet Atlanta.

"I was dancing and I went into a spin and I twisted my ankle very badly."

„Ich habe getanzt und eine schnelle Drehung gemacht, und dabei bin ich mit meinem Knöchel ziemlich böse umgeknickt."

« Je dansais, j'ai commencé une vrille et je me suis fait une vilaine entorse de la cheville. »

MICHAEL JACKSON

WEDNESDAY, MAY 12, 1993

Jackson receives awards for Best Selling United States Artist of the Year, World's Best Selling Pop and Overall Artist of the Year, and World's Best Selling Artist of the Era at the fifth annual World Music Awards, held at the Sporting Club in Monte Carlo, Monaco.

Bei der 5. Verleihung der World Music Awards im Sporting Club in Monte Carlo, Monaco, erhält Jackson die Preise als „Best Selling United States Artist of the Year", „World's Best Selling Pop and Overall Artist of the Year" und „World's Best Selling Artist of the Era".

Jackson est sacré Artiste américain le plus vendu de l'année, Meilleur chanteur du monde dans les catégories pop et générale, ainsi qu'Artiste international le plus vendu de tous les temps lors de la 5ᵉ cérémonie des World Music Awards, organisée au Sporting Club de Monte-Carlo, à Monaco.

WEDNESDAY, MAY 19, 1993
Jackson receives a Lifetime Achievement Award
from the Hollywood Guinness World of Records
Museum.

Jackson erhält den Preis für sein Lebenswerk vom
Hollywood Guinness World of Records Museum.

Le musée Guinness World of Records de Hollywood remet à Jackson un prix couronnant l'ensemble
de sa carrière.

MONDAY, AUGUST 23, 1993
A week after an investigation into charges brought
by the father of a 13-year old boy that Jackson
allegedly abused the child at his Encino home earlier
in the year begins, and two days after a raid on the
singer's Neverland Ranch, where evidence including
video tapes is removed, the Los Angeles Police
Department formally announces that Jackson is under
criminal investigation.

Eine Woche nachdem aufgrund der Anzeige des Va-
ters eines Dreizehnjährigen, der behauptete, Jackson
habe das Kind Anfang des Jahres in seinem Haus in
Encino missbraucht, polizeiliche Ermittlungen aufgenommen wurden und zwei Tage nach einer Razzia auf
der Neverland-Ranch, bei der unter anderem Video-
bänder beschlagnahmt wurden, gibt die Polizei von
Los Angeles offiziell bekannt, dass gegen Jackson kri-
minalpolizeilich ermittelt werde.

La semaine précédente, le père d'un garçon de
13 ans a porté plainte contre Jackson, qu'il accuse
d'avoir abusé de l'enfant au début de l'année, dans sa
maison d'Encino ; deux jours après avoir perquisition-
né le ranch de Neverland à la recherche de preuves,
et notamment emporté plusieurs cassettes vidéo,
la police de Los Angeles annonce officiellement que
Jackson fait l'objet d'une enquête criminelle.

TUESDAY, AUGUST 24, 1993

Confidential documents from the Los Angeles County Department of Children's Services are leaked to reporters, revealing that Dr. Evan Chandler, a Beverly Hills dentist, has claimed that his 13-year-old son, Jordan, has been sexually abused by Jackson. The boy had met Jackson the previous year, when Jackson's limousine broke down in Los Angeles, leading him to the nearest Rent-A-Wreck, where he met June Chandler, the mother of the boy. The boy had then escorted Jackson to Disney World and the World Music Awards in Monaco. As accusations fly back and forth during saturated media coverage, Jackson's private investigator, Anthony Pellicano, will publicly state that Chandler has been trying to extort $20 million from the singer and, having failed to do so, has made the accusation.

Vertrauliche Schriftstücke der Jugendfürsorge des Bezirks Los Angeles werden Reportern zugespielt. Aus ihnen geht hervor, dass Dr. Evan Chandler, ein Zahnarzt aus Beverly Hills, behauptet habe, sein dreizehnjähriger Sohn Jordan sei von Jackson sexuell missbraucht worden. Der Junge hatte Jackson im Vorjahr kennengelernt, als Jacksons Limousine in Los Angeles eine Panne hatte. Der Junge begleitete Jackson daraufhin nach Walt Disney World und zur Verleihung der World

Music Awards in Monaco. Während die gegenseitigen Anschuldigungen hin- und herfliegen und von den Medien ausgiebig verbreitet werden, gibt Anthony Pellicano, ein von Jackson engagierter Privatdetektiv, öffentlich zu Protokoll, Chandler habe zunächst versucht, den Sänger um 20 Millionen Dollar zu erpressen und habe die Anschuldigungen erst nach dem Scheitern des Erpressungsversuchs erhoben.

Des documents émanant des services sociaux du comté de Los Angeles filtrent dans la presse : ils révèlent que le Dr Evan Chandler, un dentiste de Beverly Hills, déclare que son fils de 13 ans, Jordan, a été agressé sexuellement par Jackson. Le jeune garçon a rencontré le chanteur l'année précédente, à la faveur d'un banal accident : la limousine de Jackson est tombée en panne à Los Angeles et il a dû louer une voiture dans le Rent-A-Wreck le plus proche, où il a rencontré la mère de Jordan. Jackson avait ensuite emmené le garçon avec lui à Disney World et aux World Music Awards, à Monaco. Les accusations sont proférées par les deux camps : l'enquêteur privé de Jackson déclarera que Chandler a tenté d'extorquer 20 millions de dollars à la star et qu'il a sorti la carte de l'accusation lorsque Jackson a refusé de céder à son chantage.

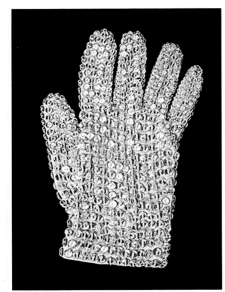

SATURDAY, AUGUST 28, 1993

Having begun the second leg of his "Dangerous" tour in Bangkok on Wednesday, and far removed from the controversy brewing in the United States, Jackson flashes a victory sign as he marches with Thai Air Force cadets.

Nachdem Jackson am Mittwoch in Bangkok die zweite Etappe seiner „Dangerous"-Tour begonnen hat und weit entfernt ist von den Kontroversen, die in den USA um seine Person entbrannt sind, zeigt er beim Marschieren mit Kadetten der thailändischen Luftwaffe mit den Fingern das V für Victory (Sieg).

Jackson a entamé la deuxième partie de sa tournée « Dangerous » à Bangkok le mercredi et, bien loin du scandale qui prend de l'ampleur aux États-Unis, il adresse un V de la victoire à la foule en défilant avec les cadets de l'armée de l'air thaïlandaise.

WEDNESDAY, SEPTEMBER 15, 1993

The day after two former Jackson employees claim they saw Jackson "doing what honeymooners do" with young boys, the alleged 13-year-old victim formally files a civil suit against the star, for seduction and sexual abuse. (Amid this controversy, Jackson will decide not to contribute the theme to the "Addams Family Values" movie.)

Einen Tag nachdem zwei frühere Angestellte Jacksons behauptet haben, sie hätten ihn mit kleinen Jungen tun sehen, „was Flitterwöchner tun", reicht sein dreizehnjähriges angebliches Opfer offiziell eine Zivilklage gegen den Star wegen Verführung Minderjähriger und sexuellen Missbrauchs ein. (Angesichts des Rechtsstreits verzichtet Jackson darauf, das Titellied zum dem Film „Addams Family Values" beizusteuern.)

La veille, deux anciens employés de Jackson ont déclaré avoir vu Jackson « faire ce qu'on fait en lune de miel » avec de jeunes garçons, et Jordan Chandler, qui se présente comme une victime de ces déviances, lance officiellement une procédure judiciaire à l'encontre de la star pour détournement de mineur et abus sexuels. (Étant donné les circonstances, Jackson décide de ne pas contribuer à la bande originale du film « Les valeurs de la famille Addams ».)

SUNDAY, NOVEMBER 14, 1993

After a much-troubled tour, which has included cancelled dates in Thailand and Singapore, apparently from the stress of the molestation charges leaving him addicted to painkillers and now rumored in the press to be undergoing alleged addiction treatment at London's Charter Nightingale clinic, Jackson's $10 million sponsorship deal with Pepsi-Cola comes to an end.

Nach einer Tour mit zahlreichen Problemen – darunter abgesagte Konzerte in Thailand und Singapur – ist Jackson von den Missbrauchsvorwürfen zusätzlich gestresst und nun offenbar von schmerzstillenden Arzneien abhängig. In der Presse werden Gerüchte verbreitet, er lasse seine Medikamentensucht in der Londoner Charter Nightingale Clinic behandeln. Sein Zehn-Millionen-Dollar-Vertrag mit Pepsi-Cola läuft aus.

Le partenariat à 10 millions de dollars avec Pepsi-Cola arrive à échéance en même temps que s'achève la tournée « Dangerous », très mouvementée. Plusieurs concerts ont été annulés en Thaïlande et à Singapour : bouleversé par les accusations de pédophilie qui pèsent contre lui, Jackson aurait trouvé refuge dans les médicaments antalgiques, et la presse affirme bientôt qu'il est entré en cure de désintoxication à la clinique Nightingale de Londres.

TUESDAY, NOVEMBER 23, 1993

After five ex-security guards at Jackson's Neverland Ranch file suit alleging that they were fired for knowing too much about Jackson's alleged fondness for young boys the previous day, Santa Monica Superior Court orders Jackson to make a deposition in reference to the civil suit, before January 31, 1994, also setting a trial date of March 21, 1994.

Nachdem ihn fünf ehemalige Sicherheitsbedienstete seiner Neverland-Ranch am Tag zuvor verklagt und berichtet haben, dass sie nur deshalb entlassen wurden, weil sie zu viel über Jacksons angebliche Vorliebe für kleine Jungen wussten, ordnet das Bezirksgericht von Santa Monica an, dass sich Jackson bis zum 31. Januar 1994 auf das anhängige Zivilverfahren einlassen müsse; die Gerichtsverhandlung wird auf den 21. März 1994 festgesetzt.

La veille, cinq anciens employés de la sécurité au ranch de Neverland ont lancé des poursuites contre Jackson, affirmant qu'ils ont été renvoyés parce qu'ils en savaient trop sur la tendresse particulière de leur patron pour les jeunes garçons. La Cour supérieure de Santa Monica ordonne au chanteur de venir témoigner dans le cadre de l'enquête avant le 31 janvier 1994, et fixe la date du procès au 21 mars 1994.

TUESDAY, NOVEMBER 30, 1993

The day after Jackson's former security guards Morris Williams and Leroy Thomas tell syndicated TV's "Hard Copy" that he frequently had children stay overnight in his room, his chauffeur makes a sworn statement that his employer had slept at least 30 straight nights at the home of the 13-year-old boy, he is alleged to have sexually abused.

Einen Tag nachdem Jacksons ehemalige Sicherheitsbedienstete Morris Williams und Leroy Thomas im landesweit ausgestrahlten amerikanischen Fernsehboulevardmagazin „Hard Copy" erzählen, er habe häufig Kinder in seinem Zimmer übernachten lassen, erklärt sein Chauffeur unter Eid, sein Arbeitgeber habe an mindestens dreißig aufeinanderfolgenden Tagen im Haus jenes dreizehnjährigen Jungen, den er angeblich sexuell missbraucht habe, übernachtet.

Au lendemain de la diffusion, dans l'émission « Hard Copy », du témoignage des anciens gardiens de Neverland Morris Williams et Leroy Thomas, racontant que Jackson invitait souvent des enfants à passer la nuit dans sa chambre, son chauffeur déclare sous serment que son patron a dormi au moins 30 fois au domicile du garçon de 13 ans qu'il est accusé d'avoir violé.

THURSDAY, DECEMBER 2, 1993

The **New York Post** and Norwalk newspaper **The Hour** report that Jackson is at the Silver Hill Hospital in New Canaan, Connecticut, a private facility that treats patients for psychiatric illnesses and substance abuse. The newspapers state that he was admitted on Monday.

Die **New York Post** und die Norwalker Zeitung **The Hour** berichten, Jackson befinde sich im Silver Hill Hospital in New Canaan, Connecticut, in einer Privatklinik für Suchtkranke und Psychiatriepatienten. Beide Zeitungen behaupten übereinstimmend, er sei am Montag eingeliefert worden.

Le **New York Post** et le journal local de Norwalk **The Hour** affirment que Jackson se trouve à l'hôpital Silver Hill de New Canaan (Connecticut), une institution privée qui traite des patients atteints d'addictions ou de troubles psychiatriques. D'après eux, il y serait entré le lundi.

WEDNESDAY, DECEMBER 8, 1993

At a press conference in Tel Aviv, Israel, estranged Jackson family member, LaToya, says of the current child-molestation allegations surrounding her brother: "I can't remain silent. I love him but I cannot and will not be a silent collaborator (in) his crimes against small innocent children. You tell me what 35-year-old man is going to take a little boy ... and stay with him for five days in his room?" (On Friday, Jackson will return to the United States aboard a private jet, amid heightened security and secrecy.)

Auf einer Pressekonferenz in Tel Aviv, Israel, kommentiert LaToya Jackson, die sich von ihrer Familie entfremdet hat, die Missbrauchsanschuldigungen gegen ihren Bruder mit den Worten: „Ich kann nicht weiter schweigen. Ich liebe ihn, aber ich kann und will keine stille Komplizin seiner Verbrechen gegen kleine,

unschuldige Kinder sein. Sagen Sie mir, welcher fünfunddreißigjährige Mann sich einen kleinen Jungen nimmt ... und fünf Tage lang mit ihm in seinem Zimmer bleibt?" (Am Freitag wird Michael Jackson in einem Privatjet mit verstärkten Sicherheitsmaßnahmen in die Vereinigten Staaten zurückkehren.)

Au cours d'une conférence de presse à Tel Aviv, LaToya Jackson réprouvée par le clan, réagit aux rumeurs qui entourent son frère : « Je ne peux pas me taire. Je l'aime, mais je ne serai pas la complice silencieuse de ses crimes contre de petits enfants innocents. Vous pouvez me dire pourquoi cet homme de 35 ans prend un petit garçon et... passe cinq jours enfermé dans une chambre avec lui ? » (Deux jours plus tard, Jackson regagne les États-Unis à bord d'un jet privé, dans le plus grand secret.)

WEDNESDAY, DECEMBER 22, 1993

Responding publicly for the first time to the current child-sex abuse allegations, Jackson holds a four-minute live satellite broadcast from the Neverland Ranch, denying everything: "I ask all of you to wait to hear the truth before you label or condemn me. Don't treat me like a criminal because I am innocent." Commenting on a body search, undertaken by the Santa Barbara and Los Angeles police departments earlier in the week, Jackson states: "They served a search warrant on me which allowed them to view and photograph my body, including my penis, my buttocks, my lower torso, thighs and any other areas that they wanted ... It was the most humiliating ordeal of my life ... I am totally innocent of any wrongdoing."

Jackson äußert sich erstmals öffentlich zu den Anschuldigungen und streitet alle Vorwürfe ab: „Ich bitte Sie alle abzuwarten, bis Sie die Wahrheit hören, bevor Sie mich abstempeln oder verdammen. Behandeln Sie mich nicht wie einen Verbrecher, denn ich bin unschuldig." Zu einer Leibesvisitation der Polizeibehörden von Santa Barbara und Los Angeles Anfang der Woche meint Jackson: „Sie zeigten mir einen Durchsuchungsbefehl, der ihnen gestattete, meinen Körper, einschließlich meines Penis, meines Gesäßes, meines Unterleibs, meiner Schenkel und beliebiger anderer Bereiche anzuschauen und zu fotografieren. ... Es war die demütigendste Quälerei meines Lebens. ... Ich bin keines Fehlverhaltens schuldig."

Dans un message de quatre minutes retransmis en direct depuis son ranch de Neverland, Jackson répond pour la première fois publiquement aux accusations de pédophilie qui pèsent contre lui, et nie tout en bloc : « Je vous demande à tous d'attendre de savoir la vérité avant de me montrer du doigt ou de me condamner. Ne me traitez pas comme un criminel, parce que je suis innocent. » À propos de la fouille corporelle opérée par des agents de la police de Santa Barbara et de Los Angeles en début de semaine, Jackson déclare : « Ils m'ont présenté un mandat qui les autorisait à regarder et à prendre en photo mon corps, y compris mon pénis, mes fesses, mon bas-ventre, mes cuisses... Je suis totalement innocent de tout méfait. »

THURSDAY, DECEMBER 16, 1993

At the end of Michael Jackson's *annus horribilis*, KEZK station manager Joe Cariffe says in an on-air editorial that the St. Louis radio station will no longer play the singer's records.

Am Ende von Michael Jacksons *annus horribilis* verkündet Joe Cariffe, der Intendant des Rundfunksenders KEZK in St. Louis, Missouri, dass sein Sender die Platten des Sängers fortan nicht mehr spielen werde.

À l'issue de cette *annus horribilis* pour Michael Jackson, le patron de la station de radio de Saint Louis KEZK, Joe Cariffe, annonce dans un éditorial que sa station ne diffusera plus les disques du chanteur.

"Not only am I presumed innocent, I am innocent."

„Ich gelte nicht nur als unschuldig, ich bin unschuldig."

« Je ne suis pas seulement présumé innocent, je suis innocent. »

MICHAEL JACKSON, JANUARY 5, 1994

TUESDAY, JANUARY 25, 1994

Jackson settles his civil suit with a multi-million dollar payment to the boy accusing him of molestation, though Jackson's lawyer Johnnie Cochran insists that the decision to head off a court case was "in no way an admission of guilt."

Jackson einigt sich in dem Zivilverfahren auf die Zahlung von mehreren Millionen Dollar an den Jungen, der ihn der sexuellen Belästigung bezichtigt hat, wobei Jacksons Anwalt Johnnie Cochran darauf besteht, die Entscheidung, die Gerichtsverhandlung abzuwenden, sei „in keiner Weise ein Schuldeingeständnis".

Jackson négocie un arrêt des poursuites judiciaires en offrant un dédommagement de plusieurs millions de dollars au garçon qui l'accuse d'abus sexuels, mais l'avocat de Jackson souligne que cet arrangement n'est en aucun cas « un aveu de culpabilité ».

THURSDAY, APRIL 28, 1994

Jackson receives the Caring For Kids' Award from Body Sculpt, an organization that uses body building to persuade children to avoid drugs and remain in school, at the Children's Choice Awards at New York's City Center.

Jackson erhält bei den Children's Choice Awards im New Yorker City Center den „Caring For Kids' Kids Award" von Body Sculpt, einer Organisation, die Kinder durch Bodybuilding stark gegen Drogenmissbrauch und vorzeitigen Schulabbruch machen möchte.

Jackson reçoit le prix des Enfants Caring For Kids de l'organisation Body Sculpt, qui utilise la musculation pour encourager les enfants à ne pas se droguer et à ne pas quitter l'école, lors de la remise des Children's Choice Awards au City Center de New York.

THURSDAY, MAY 26, 1994

Jackson and Lisa Marie Presley are married in La Vega, Dominican Republic, an event they will deny took place for more than two months. Viewed by many in the media as a loveless showbiz arrangement, Elvis' daughter will subsequently reveal that she was concerned about her husband's health in the face of the child molestation charges and his addiction to prescription drugs: "I believed he didn't do anything wrong and that he was wrongly accused and yes I started falling for him. I wanted to save him. I felt that I could do it."

Michael Jackson und Lisa Marie Presley werden in La Vega in der Dominikanischen Republik von einem Zivilrichter getraut, was sie allerdings mehr als zwei Monate lang öffentlich bestreiten. In den Medien betrachten viele diese Hochzeit als ein Arrangement, das eher ein Zugeständnis an das Showgeschäft als an die gegenseitige Liebe ist. Die Tochter von Elvis Presley erklärt später, sie habe sich angesichts der Vorwürfe des Kindesmissbrauchs und der Medikamentensucht ihres Ehemanns Sorgen um dessen Gesundheit gemacht: „Ich glaube, dass er nichts Unrechtes getan hat und dass er zu Unrecht beschuldigt wurde, und – ja, ich habe mich in ihn verliebt. Ich wollte ihn retten. Ich hatte das Gefühl, ich könnte das schaffen."

Jackson et Lisa Marie Presley sont mariés à La Vega, en République dominicaine. Pendant plus de deux mois, ils nieront que l'événement a eu lieu, et beaucoup considèrent qu'il s'agit d'un mariage arrangé. La fille d'Elvis révélera ensuite qu'elle s'inquiétait beaucoup pour la santé de son mari, profondément choqué par ses déboires judiciaires et affaibli par son addiction aux antalgiques : « Je pensais qu'il n'avait rien fait de mal et qu'il était accusé à tort et, oui, je suis tombée amoureuse de lui. Je voulais le sauver. J'ai cru que je pourrais y arriver. »

THURSDAY, SEPTEMBER 8, 1994

Newly-weds, Michael and Lisa Marie Jackson, kiss "passionately" and publicly at the 11th annual MTV Video Music Awards, emceed by Roseanne Barr, held at the Radio City Music Hall.

Das frisch vermählte Ehepaar Michael und Lisa Marie Jackson küsst sich „leidenschaftlich" und öffentlich während der 11. Verleihung der MTV Video Music

Awards in der New Yorker Radio City Music Hall, präsentiert von Roseanne Barr.

Les jeunes mariés Michael et Lisa Marie Jackson s'embrassent «passionnément», et publiquement, sur la scène des 11ᵉ MTV Video Music Awards présentés par Roseanne Barr au Radio City Music Hall de New York.

SATURDAY, OCTOBER 1, 1994

Following the announcement that the Los Angeles and Santa Barbara's District Attorney's offices will not file child molestation charges against Jackson, the **Daily Mirror** newspaper in the United Kingdom prints a color photo of the singer in scoutmaster's uniform with five other Boy Scouts. The picture is apparently from his 1995 calendar.

Nachdem bekannt gegeben wurde, dass die Staatsanwaltschaften von Los Angeles und Santa Barbara keine Anklage wegen Kindesmissbrauchs gegen Jackson erheben werden, bringt die britische Zeitung **Daily Mirror** ein Farbfoto des Sängers in der Uniform eines Pfadfinderführers, umringt von fünf männlichen Pfadfindern. Das Bild stammt offenbar aus seinem Kalender für das kommende Jahr.

Alors que le bureau du procureur des districts de Los Angeles et Santa Barbara vient d'annoncer qu'il ne poursuivra pas Jackson pour abus sexuels sur mineurs, le **Daily Mirror** publie une photo couleur du chanteur posant en uniforme de chef scout avec cinq Boy Scouts, apparemment tirée d'un calendrier de 1995.

SATURDAY, OCTOBER 8, 1994

Jackson attends the all-star "Elvis Aaron Presley— The Tribute" with Lisa Marie and sister Janet at the Pyramid Arena in Memphis, Tennessee. (Quoted in **Ebony**, Jackson reveals that when he asked Lisa Marie to marry him over the phone, she responded "Excuse me, I have to go to the bathroom".)

Mit Ehefrau Lisa Marie und Schwester Janet wohnt Michael Jackson der Veranstaltung „Elvis Aaron Presley – The Tribute" bei, einer Hommage mit zahlreichen Stars, in der Pyramid Arena in Memphis, Tennessee. (Die Zeitschrift **Ebony** zitiert Jacksons Eröffnung, auf seinen telefonischen Heiratsantrag habe Lisa Marie ihm geantwortet: „Entschuldige bitte, ich muss zur Toilette.")

Jackson assiste au concert d'hommage au King « Elvis Aaron Presley – The Tribute » avec Lisa Marie et sa sœur Janet à la Pyramid Arena de Memphis (Tennessee). (Cité par le magazine **Ebony**, Jackson raconte que, lorsqu'il a demandé à Lisa Marie de l'épouser, au téléphone, elle lui a répondu : « Excuse-moi, il faut que j'aille aux toilettes. »)

"Michael Jackson is not and has not been a registered leader or member of the Boy Scouts of America. Our approval for publication was not sought, and the publisher has not returned our phone calls."

„Michael Jackson ist und war nie als Mitglied oder Leiter bei den Boy Scouts of America eingetragen. Wir wurden nie um Einverständnis für die Veröffentlichung ersucht, und der Verleger hat unsere Anrufe nie beantwortet."

« Michael Jackson n'est pas et n'a jamais été un membre recensé des Boy Scouts d'Amérique. Personne n'a demandé notre accord avant cette publication, et l'éditeur n'a pas répondu à nos appels téléphoniques. »

THE BOY SCOUTS OF AMERICA

THURSDAY, JANUARY 12, 1995

Jackson files a $100 million lawsuit against a Los Angeles radio station and two producers of TV tabloid show "Hard Copy," alleging they slandered him when they stated there was a renewed police investigation into new allegations of child molestation.

Jackson verklagt einen Rundfunksender in Los Angeles und zwei Produzenten des Fernsehboulevardmagazins „Hard Copy" auf 100 Millionen Dollar Schadenersatz wegen Rufmords, weil sie angeblich behauptet hatten, die Polizei ermittle wieder gegen ihn wegen neuer Anschuldigungen des Kindesmissbrauchs.

Jackson attaque en justice une station de radio de Los Angeles et deux producteurs de l'émission américaine « Hard Copy », exigeant d'eux 100 millions de dollars en dommages et intérêts pour l'avoir calomnié en annonçant qu'une enquête avait été rouverte contre lui en raison de nouvelles allégations d'abus sexuels sur mineurs.

THURSDAY, FEBRUARY 23, 1995

Jackson appears at the Sony Music Distribution product presentation to herald the forthcoming release of *HIStory—Past, Present And Future Book I* at the annual NARM meeting in San Diego. He also receives the Harry Chapin Memorial Humanitarian Award.

Jackson tritt bei der Präsentation von Sony Music Distribution bei der Jahrestagung des US-Händlerverbands NARM in San Diego auf, um das Erscheinen seines nächsten Albums, *HIStory - Past, Present And*

Future Book I, anzukündigen. Außerdem erhält er den „Harry Chapin Memorial Humanitarian Award".

Jackson fait une apparition chez Sony Music Distribution pour une présentation de la stratégie commerciale qui accompagnera la sortie prochaine du premier volet de *HIStory — Past, Present And Futur* lors de la convention annuelle de la NARM, à San Diego. Il reçoit également le Harry Chapin Memorial Humanitarian Award.

TUESDAY, APRIL 18, 1995

46 children from 17 countries, as members of the World Children's Congress, visit the Neverland Ranch.

46 Kinder aus 17 Nationen besuchen die Neverland-Ranch als Mitglieder des World Children's Congress.

Une délégation de 46 enfants de 17 pays membres du Parlement mondial des enfants visite Neverland.

WEDNESDAY, JUNE 14, 1995

Jackson, with Lisa Marie by his side, is interviewed by Diane Sawyer on ABC-TV's "Primetime Live." The show posts a 60 million audience, 30 million less than viewed his Oprah Winfrey appearance.

Jackson wird mit Lisa Marie von Diane Sawyer in der Sendung „Primetime Live" interviewt. Die Sendung verzeichnet 60 Millionen Zuschauer, 30 Millionen weniger als sein Auftritt in Oprah Winfreys Talkshow.

Jackson est interviewé par Diane Sawyer pour l'émission « Primetime Live » de la chaîne ABC, avec Lisa Marie. Cet entretien est regardé par 60 millions de téléspectateurs.

THURSDAY, JUNE 15, 1995

A 10 meter high, 2,100 kilo statue of Jackson sails under Tower Bridge in London, as the worldwide hype over the double-set *HIStory—Past, Present And Future Book I* increases to fever pitch. The album—part hits and part new material—features new productions by Jam & Lewis, David Foster, R. Kelly and Dallas Austin.

Eine zehn Meter hohe und 2.100 Kilogramm schwere Jackson-Statue wird auf der Themse unter der Londoner Tower Bridge hindurchgefahren, während der weltweite Werberummel zum neuen Doppelalbum *HIStory - Past, Present And Future Book I* seinen Höhepunkt erreicht. Das Album, das zum Teil aus Hits und zum Teil aus neuem Material besteht, enthält neue Produktionen von Jam & Lewis, David Foster, R. Kelly und Dallas Austin.

Une statue monumentale de Jackson haute de dix mètres et pesant plus de deux tonnes glisse sous le Tower Bridge de Londres, dans le cadre de la campagne de promotion mondiale du premier volet de *HIStory – Past, Present And Future*, qui atteint alors son paroxysme. L'album – composé d'un mélange de vieux succès et de compositions inédites – inclut de nouvelles versions produites par Jam & Lewis, David Foster, R. Kelly et Dallas Austin.

FRIDAY, JUNE 16, 1995
Jackson releases a statement apologizing for the seemingly anti-semitic lyrics of *They Don't Care About Us*. Steven Spielberg, who has contributed glowing liner notes to *HIStory—Past, Present And Future Book I* distances himself from the controversy.

Jackson entschuldigt sich öffentlich für die judenfeindlich klingenden Textpassagen in *They Don't Care About Us*. Steven Spielberg, der noch in den Liner Notes für *HIStory - Past, Present And Future Book I* lobende Worte gefunden hatte, distanziert sich nun von der Debatte.

Jackson diffuse un communiqué dans lequel il s'excuse pour les paroles de *They Don't Care About Us* qui ont pu être jugées antisémites. Steven Spielberg, qui a rédigé une partie du livret accompagnant *HIStory — Past, Present And Future* n'intervient pas dans la polémique.

THURSDAY, JUNE 22, 1995
Jackson is honored for his Heal The World Foundation at the second annual VH-1 Honors.

Jackson wird bei der 2. Verleihung der VH 1 Honors für seine Stiftung Heal The World geehrt.

La cérémonie des VH-1 Honors rend hommage à Jackson pour le travail de sa fondation, Heal The World.

FRIDAY, JULY 28, 1995

A week after a Los Angeles Superior Court judge dismisses a suit against Jackson filed by five former security guards, citing that they signed releases barring them from talking to the press, which they have repeatedly done, ABC-TV broadcasts "Michael Jackson Changes HIStory," a half-hour special of music videos including the premiere of his new single, *You Are Not Alone.*

Eine Woche nachdem ein Richter am Bezirksgericht von Los Angeles die Klage von fünf ehemaligen Sicherheitsbediensteten gegen Jackson zurückgewiesen hat, weil diese entgegen schriftlicher Vereinbarungen wiederholt mit der Presse gesprochen haben, strahlt ABC das halbstündige Fernsehspecial „Michael Jackson Changes HIStory" aus, darunter die Premiere seines neuen Songs *You Are Not Alone.*

Une semaine plus tôt, un juge de la Cour supérieure de Los Angeles a débouté les plaintes déposées contre Jackson par cinq de ses anciens gardes du corps, arguant qu'ils avaient signé des clauses de confidentialité avec leur ancien patron, qu'ils ont consciencieusement rompues en se répandant dans la presse. Ce soir-là, ABC diffuse une émission spéciale d'une demi-heure intitulée «Michael Jackson Changes HIStory», un montage de clips musicaux parmi lesquels celui de son nouveau titre, *You Are Not Alone.*

THURSDAY, SEPTEMBER 7, 1995

Jackson lip-synchs his way through a medley of past hits and *You Are Not Alone* at the 12th annual MTV Video Music Awards from Radio City Music Hall. The lip-synching seems appropriate as legendary mime artist Marcel Marceau joins him onstage.

Bei der 12. Verleihung der MTV Video Music Awards in der New Yorker Radio City Music Hall bewegt Jackson die Lippen zum Playback eines Medleys und dem neuen Song *You Are Not Alone.* Jacksons stummer „Gesang" erscheint passend zum Auftritt des Pantomimen Marcel Marceau, der zu ihm auf die Bühne kommt.

Jackson mime un playback d'extraits de ses plus grands succès et de *You Are Not Alone* aux 12ᵉ MTV Video Music Awards, enregistrés au Radio City Music Hall. Le playback prend un sens nouveau lorsque le légendaire Marcel Marceau rejoint Jackson sur scène.

FRIDAY, SEPTEMBER 22, 1995

Jackson is the principal inductee at Black Entertainment Television's Walk of Fame in Washington, naming his contribution the most significant in the music video industry. He performs *You Are Not Alone* with the Union Temple Baptist Choir.

Jackson ist der wichtigste Neuzugang beim „Walk of Fame" des Fernsehsenders Black Entertainment Television (BET) in Washington, wo sein Beitrag als der bedeutendste in der Musikvideoindustrie gewürdigt wird. Er singt mit dem Union Temple Baptist Choir zusammen *You Are Not Alone.*

Jackson fait partie des principaux artistes inscrits au Black Entertainment Television's Walk of Fame, à Washington, qui salue son immense contribution à l'industrie de la vidéo musicale. Il interprète *You Are Not Alone* avec le Union Temple Baptist Choir.

TUESDAY, NOVEMBER 7, 1995

A week after Jackson is inducted into the Soul Train Hall of Fame at the 25th annual ceremonies, Sony releases a statement that the company has entered into a joint agreement with the singer under which he will merge his ATV publishing copyrights with theirs. Jackson receives an upfront payment reported to be between $90 and $110 million. His own MIJAC Music publishing unit stays with Warner Chappell. To celebrate the announcement, Jackson will win Best Male Performer category at the second annual MTV European Music Awards, held at Le Zenith in Paris, France at the end of the month.

Eine Woche nachdem Jackson bei der 25. Zeremonie in die Soul Train Hall of Fame aufgenommen wurde, gibt Sony bekannt, dass das Unternehmen mit dem Sänger eine Übereinkunft getroffen habe, in deren Rahmen er seine Rechte am ATV Music Publishing Catalog mit denen von Sony zusammenführen werde. Jackson erhält dafür eine Vorauszahlung, die angeblich zwischen 90 und 110 Millionen Dollar liegt. Sein eigener Musikverlag MIJAC bleibt bei Warner Chappell. Ende des Monats gewinnt Jackson bei der 2. Verleihung der MTV European Music Awards in Le Zénith in der französischen Hauptstadt den Preis in der Kategorie „Best Male Performer".

Une semaine après que Jackson a fait son entrée dans le Soul Train Hall of Fame, au cours de la 25ᵉ cérémonie annuelle, Sony diffuse un communiqué annonçant que Jackson et le pôle divertissement de la compagnie ont décidé de fusionner les droits d'auteur d'ATV et les leurs. Jackson reçoit un premier versement dont le montant se situerait entre 90 et 110 millions de dollars. Sa maison d'édition MIJAC Music demeure dans le giron de Warner Chappell. À la fin du mois, comme pour célébrer cet accord, Jackson est sacré Meilleur artiste masculin lors des seconds MTV European Music Awards au Zénith de Paris.

WEDNESDAY, DECEMBER 6, 1995

Currently enjoying his second British No. 1 of the year with *Earth Song*, Jackson collapses onstage while rehearsing for his upcoming HBO special "Michael Jackson: One Night Only" at New York's Beacon Theatre. Emergency workers find him semi-conscious lying on the side of the stage at about 5:00 p.m. EMS technician Kevin Barwick reveals 'He was lethargic. He was speaking slowly, mumbling.' EMS spokesman John Hanchar says Jackson's blood pressure was measured at 70 over 40 in the ambulance on the way to the Beth Israel Medical Center North. He undergoes tests and is treated for apparent dehydration. With Jackson in intensive care on the second floor of the hospital, surrounded by framed posters of Shirley Temple, Mickey Mouse and Topo Gigio, Dr. William Alleyne will reveal that Jackson is suffering from a viral infection and had been ill for at least a week before collapsing. He is being treated for inflammation of the stomach, dehydration and kidney and liver irregularities, caused by an electrolyte imbalance.

Während *Earth Song* als zweite seiner Singles in diesem Jahr die britischen Charts anführt, bricht Jackson auf der Bühne zusammen, als er für sein Special „Michael Jackson: One Night Only" für den Pay-TV-Sender HBO im New Yorker Beacon Theatre probt. Die Rettungskräfte finden ihn gegen 17 Uhr halb bewusstlos am Rand der Bühne. Ein Sprecher des Rettungsdienstes erklärt, Jacksons Blutdruck habe auf dem Weg zum Beth Israel Medical Center North bei 70 zu 40 gelegen. Jackson wird untersucht und wegen Dehydratation

behandelt. Er liegt auf der Intensivstation, umgeben von gerahmten Postern von Kinderstar Shirley Temple, Mickey Mouse und Topo Gigio. Dr. William Alleyne wird bekannt geben, dass Jackson unter einer Virusinfektion leide und bereits vor seinem Kollaps eine Woche lang krank gewesen sei. Er wird wegen einer Magenentzündung, Dehydratation sowie Unregelmäßigkeiten in der Funktion von Nieren und Leber behandelt, die durch Elektrolytstörungen hervorgerufen wurden.

Alors qu'il vient d'atteindre la première place des ventes britanniques pour la seconde fois de l'année avec *Earth Song*, Jackson s'effondre sur scène pendant les répétitions de la soirée spéciale programmée par la chaîne HBO, « Michael Jackson : One Night Only », au Beacon Theatre de New York. Les secours, appelés en urgence, le trouvent gisant à demi-conscient dans les coulisses aux environs de 17 h. Le porte-parole de l'équivalent américain du SAMU, John Hanchar, déclare que la tension artérielle de Jackson a été mesurée à 7/4 dans l'ambulance. Il subit divers examens et est traité pour ce qui semble être une déshydratation. Jackson est en soins intensifs au premier étage de l'hôpital, entouré d'affiches encadrées représentant Shirley Temple, Mickey Mouse et Topo Gigio. Le Dr William Alleyne annoncera qu'il souffre d'une infection virale et devait être malade depuis déjà une semaine quand il s'est évanoui. Il est soigné pour une inflammation de l'estomac, une déshydratation sévère et des dérèglements des reins et du foie provoqués par un déséquilibre électrolytique.

MONDAY, JANUARY 29, 1996

A week after Lisa Marie files for divorce in a Los Angeles court citing "irreconcilable differences," Jackson is named Favorite Pop/Rock Male Artist at the 23rd annual American Music Awards, held at the Shrine Auditorium.

Eine Woche nachdem Lisa Marie bei einem Gericht in Los Angeles wegen „unüberbrückbarer Differenzen" die Scheidung eingereicht hat, wird Jackson bei der 23. Verleihung der American Music Awards im Shrine Auditorium zum „Favorite Pop/Rock Male Artist" gekürt.

Une semaine après le dépôt d'une demande de divorce par Lisa Marie devant le tribunal de Los Angeles, en raison de «différences irréconciliables», Jackson est nommé Meilleur artiste pop/rock de l'année lors des 23ᵉ American Music Awards, au Shrine Auditorium.

MONDAY, FEBRUARY 5, 1996

Judge Luiz Haddad issues an order barring Jackson from filming in the Santa Maria shantytown in Rio de Janeiro, Brazil for 20 days, to give him time to "better explain his intentions." (He will reduce the time to five days on the 6th, with filming beginning on 12th.)

Richter Luiz Haddad verbietet Jackson für 20 Tage die Dreharbeiten in Santa Maria bei Rio de Janeiro, um ihm Zeit zu geben, „seine Absichten besser zu erklären". (Am nächsten Tag verkürzt er die Sperre auf fünf Tage, die Dreharbeiten beginnen am 12. Februar.)

Le juge Luiz Haddad interdit à Jackson de tourner dans la favela de Santa Maria à Rio de Janeiro avant un délai de 20 jours, que l'artiste devra mettre à profit pour «mieux expliquer ses intentions». (Le tournage commencera le 12.)

MONDAY, FEBRUARY 19, 1996

Jackson's performance of *Earth Song* at the 15th annual BRIT Awards at London's Earl's Court Exhibition Centre, at which he also picks up the Artist of a Generation award, is interrupted when Pulp's Jarvis Cocker walks on-stage, causing a melée during which it is claimed some of the children sharing the stage with Jackson, are injured. Cocker claims that his behavior, for which he will be arrested but not charged, was "a form of protest at the way Michael Jackson sees himself as some Christ-like figure with the power of healing." Jackson states afterwards that he was "immensely proud that the show went on despite (Cocker's) disgusting and cowardly behavior."

Während Jackson bei der 15. Verleihung der BRIT Awards im Londoner Earl's Court Exhibition Centre, wo er den „Artist of a Generation Award" entgegennimmt, seinen *Earth Song* singt, stürmt Jarvis Cocker von der Gruppe Pulp auf die Bühne. Es kommt zu einem Handgemenge, wobei einige der Kinder, die mit Jackson auf der Bühne stehen, angeblich verletzt wurden. Cocker behauptet, seine Aktion, für die er zwar

verhaftet, aber nicht vor Gericht gestellt wird, sei „eine Form des Protests gegen die Art und Weise, in der sich Michael Jackson selbst als eine Art christusähnliche Figur mit Heilkräften sieht". Jackson erklärt nach dem Auftritt, er sei „ungeheuer stolz, dass die Show trotz (Cockers) ekelhaftem und feigem Verhalten fortgesetzt wurde".

Jackson interprète *Earth Song* lors de la 15e cérémonie des BRIT Awards au Parc des expositions d'Earl's Court à Londres, quand sa prestation est interrompue par l'intrusion sur scène du chanteur de Pulp, Jarvis Cocker, qui provoque une mêlée au cours de laquelle certains des enfants présents aux côtés de Michael Jackson auraient été blessés. Cocker, qui est arrêté mais n'est pas inculpé, explique qu'il a voulu protester contre la manière dont Jackson se considère comme une sorte de Messie capable de guérir tous les maux. Jackson déclarera ensuite qu'il est «immensément fier que le spectacle ait continué malgré cette attitude répugnante et lâche». La star repart de la soirée avec le trophée d'Artiste de la génération.

TUESDAY, MARCH 19, 1996

Michael Jackson and Saudi Arabian billionaire Prince Alwaleed Bin Talal Bin Abdulaziz Alsaud hold a press conference in Paris, France, to announce their partnership in founding the Kingdom Entertainment group with the vague aim to participate in "the global multimedia explosion" and to establish projects focusing on "traditional family values."

Michael Jackson und der saudi-arabische Milliardär Prinz Alwaleed Bin Talal Bin Abdulaziz Alsaud halten in Paris eine Pressekonferenz ab, um ihre Partnerschaft bei der Gründung der Gruppe Kingdom Entertainment zu verkünden, deren vage gestecktes Ziel es ist, an der „globalen Multimediaexplosion" teilzuhaben und Projekte ins Leben zu rufen, die sich auf „traditionelle Familienwerte" konzentrieren.

Michael Jackson et le prince saoudien Alwaleed Bin Talal Bin Abdulaziz Alsaud tiennent une conférence de presse conjointe à Paris et annoncent qu'ils s'associent pour créer le groupe Kingdom Entertainment, dans le but assez vague de participer à « l'explosion mondiale du multimédia » et de monter des projets centrés sur « les valeurs familiales traditionnelles ».

FRIDAY, APRIL 12, 1996

Ex-staff members win judicial approval in Santa Barbara County Superior Court from Judge Zel Canter to proceed with a lawsuit against Jackson. They allege they were forced to quit over their refusal to say what they told a Grand Jury.

Richter Zel Canter vom Bezirksgericht Santa Barbara gestattet ehemaligen Mitarbeitern, mit einem Gerichtsverfahren gegen Jackson fortzufahren. Sie behaupten, sie seien zur Kündigung gezwungen worden, weil sie sich geweigert hatten, Jackson gegenüber ihre Aussage vor einer Grand Jury zu wiederholen.

Le juge de la Cour supérieure du comté de Santa Barbara autorise plusieurs anciens employés de Jackson à lancer une action en justice contre leur ancien patron. Ils affirment avoir été renvoyés après avoir refusé de répéter ce qu'ils avaient déclaré au Grand Jury.

TUESDAY, MAY 7, 1996

Evan Chandler files a $60 million breach of contract suit against Jackson and Lisa Marie in Santa Barbara for violating a confidentiality clause in the 1994 out-of-court settlement by discussing the case with Diane Sawyer on "Primetime Live."

Evan Chandler verklagt Jackson und Lisa Marie auf 60 Millionen Dollar, weil sie angeblich eine Vertraulichkeitsklausel der außergerichtlichen Einigung aus dem Jahre 1994 gebrochen haben, indem sie in der Sendung „Primetime Live" über den Fall sprachen.

Evan Chandler poursuit en justice Jackson et Lisa Marie et réclame 60 millions de dollars de dommages et intérêts pour rupture de contrat : il les accuse d'avoir violé la clause de confidentialité prévue dans leur accord à l'amiable de 1994.

SATURDAY, SEPTEMBER 7, 1996

Jackson embarks on the first leg of the "HIStory" world tour at the Letenska Park in Prague, the Czech Republic. Set to close on October 15 the following year, he will perform 82 concerts in 58 cities in 35 countries—his most successful tour ever.

Jackson beginnt die erste Etappe seine „HIStory"-Welttournee im Letná-Park in Prag. Bis zum 15. Oktober des nächsten Jahres plant er 82 Konzerte in 58 Städten in 35 Ländern – seine erfolgreichste Tour überhaupt.

Jackson entame la première partie de la tournée mondiale « HIStory » au Letenska Park de Prague. Elle doit se terminer le 15 octobre de l'année suivante, après 82 concerts dans 58 villes de 35 pays, et représenter l'apogée de sa carrière.

TUESDAY, OCTOBER 8, 1996

The local **Star** newspaper reports that an application for his October 27 concert in Kuala Lumpur is rejected by municipal authorities, citing "the effect it would have on the young." They had also prohibited a Jackson concert three years earlier. (The Malaysian government will give Jackson permission on the 21st.)

Die malaysische Zeitung **Star** berichtet, die Behörden von Kuala Lumpur hätten Jackson aufgrund der „Auswirkungen auf die Jugend" die Genehmigung für ein Konzert in der Stadt am 27. Oktober verweigert. Sie hatten bereits drei Jahre zuvor ein Jackson-Konzert verhindert. (Am 21. Oktober gibt die malaysische Regierung Jackson schließlich grünes Licht.)

Le journal local **Star** annonce que les autorités de Kuala Lumpur ont rejeté sa demande de concert pour le 27 octobre en raison de «l'effet qu'il pourrait avoir sur la jeunesse». Elles avaient déjà interdit un concert de Jackson trois ans plus tôt. (Le gouvernement malaysien délivrera finalement les autorisations nécessaires le 21.)

FRIDAY, OCTOBER 11, 1996

50 Christian and consumer groups protest against Jackson's concerts in South Korea because of the sex allegations brought against him.

Fünfzig christliche Gruppen und Verbrauchergruppen protestieren in Südkorea wegen der gegen Jackson erhobenen Vorwürfe der Unzucht mit Minderjährigen gegen seine Konzerte.

Cinquante groupes rassemblant chrétiens et consommateurs protestent contre les concerts de Jackson prévus en Corée-du-Sud en raison des soupçons de pédophilie qui pèsent contre lui.

TUESDAY, OCTOBER 15, 1996

Superior Court Judge Reginald Dunn rules Victor Gutierrez must pay damages to Jackson for refusing to identify the source who showed him a video of Jackson purportedly having sex with a 13-year-old boy.

Richter Reginald Dunn vom Bezirksgericht verurteilt Victor Gutierrez zu einer Schadenersatzzahlung an Jackson, weil er sich weigert, die Quelle zu nennen, von der das Video stammt, das Jackson angeblich bei sexuellen Handlungen mit einem Jungen zeigt.

Le juge de la Cour supérieure Reginald Dunn condamne Victor Gutierrez à verser des dommages et intérêts à Jackson pour avoir refusé d'identifier la personne qui lui aurait montré une vidéo dans laquelle Jackson aurait des relations sexuelles avec un garçon de 13 ans.

SATURDAY, OCTOBER 19, 1996

At a meeting to give Jackson a meritorious achievement award from the mayor of Kaohsiung, Taiwan, city councilors Huang Chao-hsing and Lin Ti-chuan burst into the room and angrily demand to know what his qualifications are for the award. Lin allegedly states "His international contribution has been to molest little boys."

Eine Zusammenkunft, in deren Verlauf der Bürgermeister der taiwanesischen Stadt Kaohsiung Jackson eine Ehrung für „anerkennenswerte Leistungen" zukommen lassen möchte, wird von den Stadträten Huang Chao-hsing und Lin Ti-chuan gestört, die aufgebracht Auskunft darüber verlangen, womit sich Jackson die Würdigung verdient habe.

La cérémonie au cours de laquelle le maire de Kaohsiung, à Taiwan, doit remettre à Jackson un prix du Mérite est interrompue par deux conseillers municipaux, qui font irruption dans la salle et exigent de savoir quelles sont ses qualifications pour mériter cet honneur.

THURSDAY, NOVEMBER 14, 1996

After the previous week's statement that Jackson's long-time girlfriend Debbie Rowe is pregnant, amid reports that she was allegedly being paid $528,000 to have the baby by way of artificial insemination, the couple marry in a private ceremony at the Sheraton on the Park Hotel in Sydney, Australia at approximately 2:00 a.m. after a concert at the Sydney Cricket Ground. Jackson will say "I am thrilled that I will soon be a father and am looking forward, with great anticipation, to having this child. Please respect my privacy and that of Debbie and the child. This is my dream come true." The **Daily Mirror** reports that Jackson signed a deal with Rowe which will pay her $1.25 million when the child is born and $280,000 a year for every year the couple is married after that and that he would pay her $2.3 million if the marriage fails. (Elton John will subsequently say on the "Rosie O'Donnell" show that Australia is where "all the loonies get married".)

Nachdem eine Woche zuvor bekannt wurde, dass Jacksons langjährige Freundin Debbie Rowe schwanger ist und Gerüchte die Runde machen, sie habe 528.000 Dollar für eine künstliche Befruchtung erhalten, heiratet das Paar in kleinem Kreis im Hotel Sheraton on the Park in Sydney, Australien. Jackson erklärt später: „Ich freue mich riesig, dass ich bald Vater sein werde, und ich sehe diesem Kind mit großer Erwartung entgegen. Bitte respektieren Sie meine Privatsphäre und die Debbies und des Kindes. Dies ist für mich ein Traum, der Wirklichkeit wird." Der **Daily Mirror** berichtet, Jackson habe mit Rowe einen Vertrag geschlossen, nach dem sie 1,25 Millionen Dollar bei der Geburt des Kindes erhält und jährlich 280.000 Dollar für jedes vollendete Ehejahr sowie 2,3 Millionen Dollar im Falle einer Scheidung. (Elton John wird später in der „The Rosie O'Donnell Show" erzählen, Australien sei das Land, in dem „alle Bekloppten heiraten".)

La semaine précédente, l'entourage de Jackson a annoncé que la petite amie de longue date du chanteur, Debbie Rowe, est enceinte ; la presse parle aussitôt d'un accord financier selon lequel elle aurait touché 528 000 dollars pour concevoir le bébé par insémination artificielle. Ce même jeudi, aux environs de 2 heures du matin, à l'issue du concert de Sidney, le couple se marie dans la plus stricte intimité à l'hôtel Sheraton on the Park. Jackson déclare : « Je suis très heureux à l'idée d'être bientôt père et je suis très impatient d'avoir cet enfant. S'il vous plaît, respectez ma vie privée, celle de Debbie et de l'enfant. Mon rêve devient réalité. » Le **Daily Mirror** annonce que Jackson a signé un contrat avec Rowe, en vertu duquel il lui verserait 1,25 million de dollars à la naissance de l'enfant, puis 280 000 dollars par année de mariage, et 2,3 millions de dollars au cas où ce mariage serait un échec.

SATURDAY, JANUARY 4, 1997

The first leg of the "HIStory" world tour comes to an end at the Aloha Stadium in Honolulu, Hawaii, before a sellout crowd 35,000. (Jackson has played 42 dates in 26 cities and 20 countries, attended by more than 1.9 million fans.)

La première étape de la tournée mondiale « HIStory » s'achève à l'Aloha Stadium d'Honolulu (Hawaï) devant une foule de 35 000 spectateurs. (Plus de 1,9 million de fans ont assisté aux 42 concerts dans 26 villes de 20 pays.)

Jackson schließt vor 35.000 Konzertbesuchern die erste Etappe seiner „HIStory"-Welttournee im ausverkauften Aloha-Stadion von Honolulu, Hawaii, ab. (Bisher hat er 42 Konzerte in 26 Städten und 20 Ländern gegeben, die von insgesamt 1,9 Millionen Fans besucht wurden.)

WEDNESDAY, FEBRUARY 12, 1997

Jackson becomes a father when his wife Debbie gives birth to a boy, to be named Prince Michael, at Cedars-Sinai Medical Center in Los Angeles. (The **National Enquirer** will pay $2 million for the exclusive North American rights to the photos of the baby.)

Jackson wird Vater, als seine Frau Debbie im Cedars-Sinai Medical Center von Los Angeles einen Jungen zur Welt bringt, der den Namen Prince Michael erhält. (Das Boulevardblatt **National Enquirer** zahlt zwei Millionen Dollar für die nordamerikanischen Exklusivrechte an den Fotos des Neugeborenen.)

Debbie Jackson donne naissance à un garçon prénommé Prince Michael au centre médical Cedars-Sinai de Los Angeles : Michael Jackson est papa. (Le **National Enquirer** débourse deux millions de dollars pour obtenir l'exclusivité en Amérique du Nord sur les photos du bébé.)

SATURDAY, APRIL 19, 1997
A wax museum statue of Jackson, for which he posed, is unveiled at Paris' Grevin Museum of Wax.

Im Pariser Wachsfigurenkabinett Musée Grévin wird eine Jackson-Nachbildung enthüllt, für die er persönlich Modell gestanden hat.

Un personnage de cire de Jackson, pour lequel il a posé, est dévoilé au musée Grévin de Paris.

TUESDAY, MAY 6, 1997
The Jackson 5 are inducted into the Rock and Roll Hall of Fame at the 12th annual induction dinner, hosted for the first time at the Rock and Roll Hall of Fame Museum in Cleveland, Ohio.

Die Jackson 5 werden beim 12. Jahresdinner, das erstmals im Rock and Roll Hall of Fame Museum in Cleveland, Ohio, stattfindet, in die Rock and Roll Hall of Fame aufgenommen.

Les Jackson 5 entrent au Rock and Roll Hall of Fame lors de la 12ᵉ cérémonie d'intronisation de l'association, qui se tient pour la première fois dans le musée du Rock and Roll Hall of Fame, à Cleveland (Ohio).

"He is an artist totally fascinated by his own image."

„Er ist ein Künstler, der von seinem eigenen Bild völlig fasziniert ist."

« C'est un artiste totalement fasciné par sa propre image. »

SCULPTOR DENIS LONGCHAMPT

MONDAY, JULY 7, 1997
Thriller becomes the first record to sell in excess of 25 million copies in the United States. (It will go on to be the best-selling album of all time worldwide.)

Thriller devient le premier disque à s'être vendu à plus de 25 millions d'exemplaires aux États-Unis. (Il demeure d'ailleurs l'album le plus acheté dans le monde.)

Thriller wird die erste Platte, von der in den Vereinigten Staaten mehr als 25 Millionen Exemplare verkauft werden. (Weltweit wird sie zum meistverkauften Album aller Zeiten.)

MONDAY, FEBRUARY 23, 1998

Two days before attending the inauguration of president-elect Kim Dae Jung in Seoul, South Korea, Jackson visits the country's largest amusement park, Everland, in Yongin. The previous week, he had won approval from Polish authorities to build a $500 million 222-acre amusement park in Warsaw.

Zwei Tage bevor er der Amtseinführung des neu gewählten Präsidenten Kim Dae Jung in der südkoreanischen Hauptstadt Seoul beiwohnt, besucht Jackson Everland, den größten Vergnügungspark des Landes, in Yongin. In der Vorwoche war ihm von polnischen Behörden die Genehmigung zum Bau eines 90 Hektar großen und 500 Millionen Dollar teuren Vergnügungsparks in Warschau erteilt worden.

Deux jours avant d'assister à la cérémonie d'investiture du président sud-coréen Kim Dae Jung à Séoul, Jackson visite le plus grand parc à thème du pays, Everland, à Yongin. La semaine précédente, les autorités polonaises l'ont autorisé à construire un parc semblable sur un terrain de 111 hectares à Varsovie, pour un budget de 500 millions de dollars.

FRIDAY, MAY 15, 1998

Jackson, who became a father for the second time the previous month when Debbie Rowe gave birth to their second child, a 7lb 9 oz girl, to be named Paris Michael Katherine Jackson, in Beverly Hills, holds a press conference at the Beverly Hilton Hotel to announce a series of worldwide benefit concerts for

children. The first will be on October 11 in Seoul with Luciano Pavarotti and Elizabeth Taylor. On Sunday, he will meet Namibian president Sam Nujoma in Windhoek at the World Economic Forum, as he announces plans to build a leisure complex and shopping centers in the impoverished country.

Jackson, der im Vormonat zum zweiten Mal Vater geworden ist, als ihm Debbie Rowe in Beverly Hills ein Mädchen gebar, das den Namen Paris Michael Katherine Jackson trägt, hält im Beverly Hilton Hotel eine Pressekonferenz ab, in der er Benefizkonzerte für Kinder ankündigt. Das erste werde am 11. Oktober mit Luciano Pavarotti und Elizabeth Taylor in Seoul stattfinden. Am Sonntag wird er sich mit dem namibischen Präsidenten Sam Nujoma in Windhuk beim Weltwirtschaftsforum treffen und verkünden, in dem verarmten Land eine Freizeitanlage und Einkaufszentren zu bauen.

Jackson, devenu père pour la deuxième fois un mois plus tôt, lorsque Debbie Rowe a donné naissance à Beverly Hills à une petite fille prénommée Paris Michael Katherine Jackson, tient une conférence de presse au Beverly Hilton Hotel pour annoncer une série de concerts caritatifs au profit des enfants. Le premier aura lieu le 11 octobre à Séoul, avec Luciano Pavarotti et Elizabeth Taylor. Le dimanche suivant, Jackson rencontre le président namibien Sam Nujoma à Windhoek pendant le Forum économique mondial, et annonce son projet de bâtir un complexe de loisirs et des centres commerciaux dans ce pays.

TUESDAY, JULY 7, 1998

Jackson announces plans for a 75-acre Majestic Kingdom, complete with Thriller Theme Park, 800-room hotel, casino and underground aquarium in Detroit.

Jackson verkündet seine Pläne für ein 30 Hektar großes „Majestic Kingdom" in Detroit, das einen Thriller-Themenpark, ein Hotel mit 800 Zimmern, ein Casino und ein unterirdisches Aquarium umfassen soll.

Jackson annonce un projet pharaonique: Majestic Kingdom, un complexe de 38 hectares installé à Detroit qui comprendra un parc à thème «Thriller», un hôtel de 800 chambres, un casino et un aquarium sous-terrain.

MONDAY, NOVEMBER 9, 1998

Jackson settles a High Court action over articles published in the **Daily Mirror** alleging that his face was hideously disfigured and scarred as a result of cosmetic surgery. Jackson wins an apology, with his solicitor Marcus Barclay saying litigation had been settled "amicably."

Jackson legt eine Klage gegen den **Daily Mirror** bei, der in mehreren Artikeln behauptet hatte, Jacksons Gesicht sei als Folge kosmetischer Chirurgie abscheulich entstellt und vernarbt. Die Zeitung entschuldigt sich bei Jackson, und sein Anwalt Marcus Barclay erklärt, man habe sich „freundschaftlich" geeinigt.

Jackson avait attaqué en justice le **Daily Mirror**, qui avait affirmé dans plusieurs articles que son visage était déformé et couvert de cicatrices en raison de trop nombreuses opérations de chirurgie esthétique. Il obtient ce jour-là des excuses publiques, et son avocat Marcus Barclay déclare que le litige a été réglé «à l'amiable».

TUESDAY, NOVEMBER 17, 1998

Jackson meets secretly with Zimbabwe President Robert Mugabe in Harare to discuss plans for Jackson to invest in a hotel development in Victoria Falls. He also attends a cocktail party hosted by Zimbabwe Defense Industries.

Jackson trifft sich in Harare heimlich mit dem Präsidenten von Simbabwe, Robert Mugabe, um über Jacksons Pläne zu sprechen, in einen Hotelneubau in Victoria Falls zu investieren. Außerdem ist er auf einer Cocktailparty zu Gast, die von der Rüstungsindustrie des Landes ausgerichtet wird.

Jackson rencontre en secret le président du Zimbabwe Robert Mugabe à Harare pour discuter avec lui de son envie d'investir dans le développement du secteur hôtelier à Victoria Falls. Il assiste aussi à un cocktail organisé par le complexe militaire étatique Zimbabwe Defense Industries.

SUNDAY, JUNE 27, 1999

After being treated at Cedars Medical Center in Miami, Florida for a broken wrist at the beginning of the year while working on tracks for a new album, Jackson is rushed to hospital following his performance at Munich's Olympic Stadium with exhaustion. Diagnosed with a "circulatory collapse" he will be discharged in the early hours of the following day.

Anfang des Jahres wurde Jackson wegen eines gebrochenen Handgelenks während der Vorbereitungen für sein neues Album im Cedars Medical Center in Miami, Florida, behandelt. Nun wird er nach seinem Auftritt im Münchner Olympiastadion wegen Erschöpfung behandelt und ins Krankenhaus eingeliefert. Dort stellen die Ärtze einen „Kreislaufkollaps" fest, und Jackson wird in den frühen Morgenstunden des nächsten Tages entlassen.

Jackson est hospitalisé d'urgence après son concert au Stade olympique de Munich, dans un état d'épuisement général. Les médecins diagnostiquent un collapsus cardio-vasculaire, mais le laissent sortir avant l'aube. (Quelques mois plus tôt, il a déjà séjourné au Cedars Medical Center de Miami après s'être cassé le poignet alors qu'il travaillait à son nouvel album.)

SATURDAY, SEPTEMBER 4, 1999

Jackson presents Nelson Mandela with a check for one million rand ($164,000) for the Nelson Mandela Children's Fund at the 1999 Kora All Africa Music Awards at Sun City in South Africa. In return, he is presented with a Lifetime Achievement Award from Namibian Prime Minister, Hage Geingob.

Jackson übergibt Nelson Mandela während der Verleihung der Kora All Africa Music Awards in Sun City, Südafrika, einen Scheck über eine Million Rand (164.000 Dollar) für den Nelson Mandela Children's Fund. Im Gegenzug erhält er von Hage Geingob, dem Premierminister Namibias, den Preis für sein Lebenswerk.

Jackson remet à Nelson Mandela un chèque d'un million de rands (soit environ 164 000 dollars) au profit du Nelson Mandela Children's Fund à l'occasion des Kora All Africa Music Awards organisés à Sun City, en Afrique du Sud. Il reçoit aussi un prix saluant l'ensemble de sa carrière des mains du Premier ministre namibien Hage Geingob.

THE 2000^S

DIE 2000ER

LES ANNÉES 2000

MONDAY, JANUARY 17, 2000

At the 27th annual American Music Awards at the Shrine Auditorium, Jackson is named "Artist of the '80s" from an online poll: Other Artists of the Decades—Elvis Presley (1950s), the Beatles (1960s), Stevie Wonder (1970s) and Garth Brooks (1990s).

Bei der 27. Verleihung der American Music Awards im Shrine Auditorium wird Jackson auf der Grundlage einer Internetumfrage zum „Artist of the '80s" gekürt. Die anderen Auszeichnungen als „Artists of the Decade" gehen an Elvis Presley (1950er), die Beatles (1960er), Stevie Wonder (1970er) und Garth Brooks (1990er).

À l'occasion des 27e American Music Awards au Shrine Auditorium, Jackson reçoit le trophée d'Artiste de la décennie 1980, désigné après un sondage en ligne:

les autres artistes ainsi honorés sont Elvis Presley (années 1950), les Beatles (années 1960), Stevie Wonder (années 1970) et Garth Brooks (années 1990).

THURSDAY, MAY 11, 2000

Jackson performs at the World Music Awards ceremony in Monaco, as he adds a further trophy to his awards cabinet.

Jackson tritt bei der Verleihung der World Music Awards in Monaco auf und gewinnt dort eine weitere Auszeichnung für seinen Trophäenschrank.

Jackson participe à la cérémonie des World Music Awards à Monaco, et ajoute un nouveau trophée à son imposante collection.

"I would therefore like to propose tonight that we install in every home a Children's Universal Bill of Rights, the tenets of which are: 1—The right to be loved without having to earn it, 2—The right to be protected, without having to deserve it, 3—The right to feel valuable, even if you came into the world with nothing, 4—The right to be listened to without having to be interesting, 5—The right to be read a bedtime story, without having to compete with the evening news, 6—The right to an education without having to dodge bullets at schools, 7—The right to be thought of as adorable, even if you have a face that only a mother could love."

„Ich möchte deshalb heute Abend vorschlagen, dass wir in jedem Zuhause eine universelle Charta der Grundrechte des Kindes verwirklichen, die folgende Rechte festschreibt: 1. das Recht, geliebt zu werden, ohne es sich erwerben zu müssen; 2. das Recht, geschützt zu werden, ohne es verdienen zu müssen; 3. das Recht, sich als wertvoll zu empfinden, auch wenn man mit nichts zur Welt kam; 4. das Recht, ein offenes Ohr zu finden, ohne dass man etwas Interessantes mitzuteilen haben muss; 5. das Recht, eine Gute-Nacht-Geschichte vorgelesen zu bekommen, ohne in Konkurrenz zu den Abendnachrichten treten zu müssen; 6. das Recht auf Bildung, ohne dass man in der Schule Kugeln ausweichen muss; 7. das Recht, als bezaubernd zu gelten, auch wenn man ein Gesicht besitzt, das nur eine Mutter lieben könnte."

« Ce soir, j'aimerais vous proposer que nous instaurions dans chaque foyer une Charte universelle des droits de l'Enfant, dont les préceptes seront : 1 – Le droit d'être aimé sans avoir à le mériter, 2 – Le droit d'être protégé sans devoir le mériter, 3 – Le droit de se sentir précieux, même si l'on vient au monde sans rien, 4 – Le droit d'être écouté, sans devoir être intéressant, 5 – Le droit de se faire raconter une histoire avant de dormir, sans devoir concurrencer le journal télévisé, 6 – Le droit à l'éducation sans avoir à éviter les balles pour atteindre l'école, 7 – Le droit d'être trouvé adorable, même si l'on a un visage que seule une mère peut aimer. »

MICHAEL JACKSON, THE OXFORD UNION SOCIETY, MARCH 6, 2001

MONDAY, MARCH 19, 2001

Jackson is inducted by *NSync into the Rock and Roll Hall of Fame at the 16th annual dinner, held at the Waldorf-Astoria Hotel in New York City, his second such induction following the previous honor as a member of the Jackson 5. Supporting himself with a cane after recently breaking his foot, he gives a typically brief speech, thanking the Jackson 5, his parents, Berry Gordy Jr. and Diana Ross.

Jackson wird beim 16. Jahresdinner im New Yorker Hotel Waldorf-Astoria von der Gruppe *NSync in die Rock and Roll Hall of Fame eingeführt – zum zweiten Mal, nachdem er bereits als Mitglied der Jackson 5 dort vertreten ist. Jackson, der sich kurz vorher den

Fuß gebrochen hat, stützt sich auf einem Stock ab und hält eine für ihn typische kurze Dankesrede, in der er den Jackson 5, seinen Eltern, Berry Gordy Jr. und Diana Ross dankt.

Jackson est investi par *NSync au Rock and Roll Hall of Fame lors du 16ᵉ dîner annuel organisé à l'hôtel Waldorf-Astoria de New York, à titre personnel cette fois. (Il était déjà inscrit depuis peu au panthéon du rock avec les Jackson 5). Jackson, qui s'est récemment cassé le pied, s'appuie sur une canne pour rejoindre l'estrade et prononce quelques mots seulement pour remercier les Jackson 5, ses parents, Berry Gordy Jr et Diana Ross.

THURSDAY, SEPTEMBER 6, 2001

As *NSync reach the end of their performance of *Pop*, at the 18th annual MTV Awards, held at New York's Metropolitan Opera House, their etch-a-sketch backdrop flies out to reveal Jackson. He begins to dance to a Justin Timberlake beatbox accompaniment.

Am Ende des Auftritts von *NSync mit *Pop* während der 18. Verleihung der MTV Awards im New Yorker Metropolitan Opera House fliegt die Kulisse davon

und gibt den Blick auf Jackson frei. Mit einer Beatbox-Begleitung von Justin Timberlake beginnt er zu tanzen.

Alors que le groupe *NSync arrive au terme de son interprétation de *Pop*, pendant la 18ᵉ cérémonie des MTV Awards à New York, l'ardoise magique géante qui décore le fond de scène se soulève, révélant la silhouette de Jackson qui se met à danser, accompagné par Justin Timberlake.

FRIDAY, SEPTEMBER 7, 2001 & MONDAY, SEPTEMBER 10, 2001

Jackson performs two self-tribute concerts at Madison Square Garden, ostensibly staged to celebrate 30 years as a solo artist (though really to prop up interest in his upcoming album **Invincible**.) The all-star spectaculars feature special guests, the Jacksons, Whitney Houston, Britney Spears, Monica, Al Jarreau, Gladys Knight, Usher, Luther Vandross, Dionne Warwick, Liza Minnelli, Marc Anthony, *NSync, Shaggy, Slash and teen country star Billy Gilman, among others.

Jackson gibt zwei Konzerte im Madison Square Garden, angeblich zur Feier seines 30. Jahrestages als Solokünstler (tatsächlich jedoch, um Interesse für sein Album **Invincible** zu wecken). Als Gäste treten unter anderem die Jacksons, Whitney Houston, Britney Spears, Monica, Al Jarreau, Gladys Knight, Usher, Luther Vandross, Dionne Warwick, Liza Minnelli, Marc Anthony, *NSync, Shaggy, Slash und Billy Gilman auf.

Jackson donne deux concerts au Madison Square Garden. Ces deux dates sont censées célébrer ses 30 ans de carrière solo, mais elles préparent en fait la sortie de son prochain album, **Invincible**. Ces deux soirées se veulent exceptionnelles, avec la participation d'une pléiade d'invités comme les Jackson, Whitney Houston, Britney Spears, Monica, Al Jarreau, Gladys Knight, Usher, Luther Vandross, Dionne Warwick, Liza Minnelli, Marc Anthony, *NSync, Shaggy, Slash et Billy Gilman.

SUNDAY, OCTOBER 21, 2001

Jackson takes part in "United We Stand"—a 9/11 fundraising concert staged at Washington, DC's RFK Stadium. All proceeds are benefitting the Salvation Army Relief Fund, the American Red Cross, the Liberty Relief Fund, the Pentagon Relief Fund and the Rewards for Justice Fund.

Jackson beteiligt sich an „United We Stand", einem Benefizkonzert im RFK-Stadion in Washington, D.C., für die Opfer der Anschläge vom 11. September. Der Erlös kommt dem Hilfsfonds der Heilsarmee, dem Amerikanischen Roten Kreuz, dem Liberty Relief Fund, dem Pentagon Relief Fund und dem Rewards for Justice Fund zugute.

Jackson participe à «United We Stand» – un concert caritatif organisé pour les victimes des attentats du 11 septembre au RFK Stadium de Washington. Toutes les recettes sont reversées au Fonds d'intervention d'urgence de l'Armée du Salut, à la Croix-Rouge américaine, et aux fondations Liberty Relief, Pentagon Relief et Rewards for Justice.

WEDNESDAY, JANUARY 9, 2002

22 years since Jackson received the first of his 22 American Music Awards, Jackson is named Artist of the Century. In accepting the honor, he thanks Diana Ross, Marlon Brando and Gladys Knight, among others.

22 ans après avoir reçu le premier de ses 22 American Music Awards, Jackson est sacré Artiste du Siècle. Lorsqu'il vient accepter son trophée, il remercie, entre autres, Diana Ross, Marlon Brando et Gladys Knight.

22 Jahre nachdem er den ersten seiner 22 American Music Awards erhalten hat, wird Jackson zum „Artist of the Century" gekürt. Als er die Auszeichnung entgegennimmt, dankt er unter anderem Diana Ross, Marlon Brando und Gladys Knight.

SATURDAY, APRIL 20, 2002

After recently becoming a father for the third time with the birth of Prince Michael Jackson II by an unnamed surrogate mother, who has conceived the child via artificial insemination, Jackson performs *Dangerous* on "American Bandstand 50th—A Celebration" from Pasadena.

Nachdem ihn eine künstlich befruchtete, ungenannte Leihmutter mit der Geburt von Prince Michael Jackson II kürzlich zum dritten Mal zum Vater gemacht hat, singt Jackson *Dangerous* in Pasadena während der Veranstaltung „American Bandstand 50th – A Celebration".

Jackson est père pour la troisième fois : une mère porteuse (dont l'identité demeure secrète) a donné naissance à Prince Michael Jackson II, conçu par insémination artificielle. Jackson interprète *Dangerous* pour « American Bandstand 50th – A Celebration » enregistrée à Pasadena.

WEDNESDAY, APRIL 24, 2002

Jackson performs at "A Night At The Apollo," a fundraiser for the Democratic National Committee's Every Vote Counts campaign, at the legendary Apollo Theater in Harlem, New York. Red Hot Chili Pepper Dave Navarro joins him on *Black Or White*.

Jackson tritt bei „A Night At The Apollo", einer Spendensammelaktion der Kampagne „Jede Stimme zählt" des Nationalkomitees der Demokratischen Partei im legendären Apollo Theater in Harlem, New York, auf. Dave Navarro von den Red Hot Chili Peppers begleitet ihn bei *Black Or White*.

Jackson participe au concert « A Night At The Apollo », dont l'ambition est de lever des fonds pour la campagne Every Vote Counts du comité national démocrate (DNC), au légendaire Apollo Theater de Harlem, à New York. Dave Navarro des Red Hot Chili Peppers, le rejoint sur scène pour *Black Or White*.

FRIDAY, JUNE 14, 2002

During a visit to England, Jackson lambasts Sony Music chief Tommy Mottola at a charity event for third division Exeter City Football Club (where he is made an honorary director of the club.) Tomorrow he will go on another verbal rampage, calling Mottola the "Devil." Speaking to some 2,000-plus fans at the Equinox nightclub in London's Leicester Square, Jackson says "Mariah Carey, after divorcing Tommy, came to me crying. Crying. She was crying so badly I had to hold her. She said to me 'This is an evil man, and Michael, this man follows me.' He taps her phones, and he's very, very evil. She doesn't trust him." (Carey will distance herself from Jackson's comments.)

Während eines Englandbesuchs erhebt Jackson bei einer Wohltätigkeitsveranstaltung für den Drittliga-Fußballverein Exeter City, der ihn zum Ehrendirektor ernannt hat, schwere Vorwürfe gegen Tommy Mottola, den Chef von Sony Music. Am nächsten Tag wird er sich vor rund 2.000 Fans im Nachtclub Equinox am Londoner Leicester Square einen weiteren verbalen Amoklauf leisten, indem er Mottola als „Teufel" bezeichnet und behauptet: „Nachdem sich Mariah Carey von Tommy scheiden ließ, kam sie heulend zu mir. Heulend. Sie heulte so schrecklich, dass ich sie halten musste. Sie sagte zu mir: ‚Das ist ein böser Mensch' und ‚Michael, dieser Mann verfolgt mich.' Er zapft ihre Telefone an, und er ist sehr, sehr böse. Sie traut ihm nicht." (Carey wird sich später von Jacksons Behauptungen distanzieren.)

Pendant un séjour en Angleterre, Jackson s'en prend violemment au patron de Sony Music, Tommy Mottola, au cours d'un événement caritatif organisé pour le club de football de troisième division d'Exeter City (dont il est nommé président d'honneur). Il réitère sa sortie le lendemain, qualifiant Mottola de « diable ». S'adressant aux quelque 2000 fans présents dans la boîte de nuit londonienne Equinox, sur Leicester Square, Jackson lance : « Après avoir divorcé de Tommy, Mariah Carey est venue me voir en larmes. En larmes ! Elle pleurait tant que j'ai dû la prendre dans mes bras. Elle m'a dit : "C'est un homme mauvais, et Michael, cet homme me suit". Il a mis ses téléphones sur écoute et il est très, très méchant. Elle ne lui fait pas confiance. » (Carey ne confirmera pas ces déclarations.)

"And being the artist that I am, at Sony I've generated several billion dollars for Sony, several billion. They really thought that my mind is always on music and dancing ... I just owe Sony one more album, it's just a box set, really. So I'm leaving Sony a free agent, owning half of Sony. And I'm leaving them, and they are very angry because they never thought that this performer, myself, would out-think them."

„Und als der Künstler, der ich nun einmal bin, habe ich für Sony mehrere Milliarden Dollar eingespielt, mehrere Milliarden. Sie dachten wirklich, in meinem Kopf drehe sich alles immer nur um Musik und Tanz ... Ich schulde Sony nur noch ein weiteres Album, wirklich nur ein Box-Set. Also verlasse ich Sony als freier Künstler, dem die Hälfte von Sony gehört. Und ich verlasse sie, und sie sind sehr verärgert, weil sie nie gedacht hätten, dass dieser Künstler, also meine Wenigkeit, weiter denkt als sie selbst."

« Étant donné l'artiste que je suis, chez Sony j'ai généré plusieurs milliards de dollars, je leur ai rapporté plusieurs milliards. Ils pensaient vraiment que je ne m'intéressais qu'à la musique et à la danse... Je ne dois plus qu'un album à Sony, juste un coffret, en fait. Je quitte donc Sony libre comme l'air, avec la moitié de Sony dans ma poche. Je les quitte et ils sont furieux parce qu'ils n'auraient jamais cru que moi, un simple artiste, je devancerais leur stratégie. »

MICHAEL JACKSON, JUNE 15, 2002

THURSDAY, AUGUST 29, 2002

At the 19th annual MTV Video Music Awards in New York, Jackson is introduced by Britney Spears, who she calls her artist of the millennium. He says "When I was a little boy in Indiana, if someone had told me that one day I would be getting as a musician the artist of the millennium award, I wouldn't have believed this. This is really amazing. I can't believe it." Neither do MTV, who have given him no such award.

Bei der 19. Verleihung der MTV Video Music Awards wird Jacksons Auftritt von Britney Spears eingeleitet, die ihn als ihren Künstler des Jahrtausends bezeichnet. Er sagt daraufhin: „Als ich ein kleiner Junge war, hätte ich es nie geglaubt, wenn mir jemand erzählt hätte,

dass ich eines Tages als Musiker den Preis als Künstler des Jahrtausends erhalten würde. Fantastisch. Ich kann es nicht glauben." MTV kann es auch nicht glauben, denn einen solchen Preis hat man ihm nie verliehen.

Aux 19ᵉ MTV Video Music Awards, à New York, Jackson est accueilli sur scène par Britney Spears, qui déclare qu'il est son artiste préféré du millénaire. Un peu perdu, Jackson s'approche du micro : « Si on m'avait dit, quand je n'étais qu'un petit garçon de l'Indiana, qu'un jour je serai le musicien sacré Artiste du millénaire, je n'y aurais pas cru. C'est vraiment extraordinaire. Je n'arrive pas à y croire. » MTV non plus, qui ne lui a encore jamais remis un tel trophée.

"I made a terrible mistake. I got caught up in the excitement of the moment. I would never intentionally endanger the lives of my children."

„Ich habe einen furchtbaren Fehler gemacht. Ich war in diesem Augenblick so mitgerissen von der ganzen Aufregung. Ich würde niemals absichtlich das Leben meiner Kinder in Gefahr bringen."

« J'ai commis une terrible erreur. Je me suis laissé emporter par l'excitation du moment. Je ne mettrais jamais en danger la vie de mes enfants. »

MICHAEL JACKSON, NOVEMBER 20, 2002

TUESDAY, NOVEMBER 19, 2002

In a year which has witnessed increasingly bizarre behavior, Jackson appears on the balcony outside his fifth-floor room at the Adlon Hotel in Berlin, Germany and dangles his 9-month-old son Prince Michael II (aka "Blanket"—Jackson's third child who was born to an unidentified surrogate mother earlier in the year,) whose head is covered with a towel, over the railings. Jackson—taking a break from the $21 million lawsuit being heard in a California courtroom—is in Germany to pick up a Bambi Award for Lifetime Achievement.

Gegen Ende eines Jahres, in dem Jacksons Verhalten immer bizarrere Züge angenommen hat, erscheint Jackson auf dem Balkon seines Zimmers im fünften Stock des Berliner Hotels Adlon und hält seinen neun Monate alten Sohn Prince Michael II (alias „Blanket" – Jacksons drittes Kind), dessen Kopf mit einem Handtuch

bedeckt ist, über die Brüstung. Jackson, der sich gerade eine Pause von der 21-Millionen-Dollar-Klage gönnt, die derzeit vor einem kalifornischen Gericht verhandelt wird, hält sich in Deutschland auf, um sich den Bambi für sein Lebenswerk abzuholen.

Jackson, dont le comportement est de plus en plus bizarre depuis le début de l'année, apparaît au balcon de sa chambre, située au quatrième étage de l'Adlon Hotel à Berlin et brandit son dernier né de 9 mois, Prince Michael II, couvert d'une serviette (il est né d'une mère porteuse et surnommé « Blanket » – couverture) au-dessus du vide pour le présenter à la foule. Jackson, qui s'offre un changement d'air alors qu'un procès pour 21 millions de dollars est en cours en Californie, est en Allemagne pour recevoir le prix Bambi pour l'ensemble de sa carrière.

MONDAY, FEBRUARY 3, 2003

ITV in the United Kingdom airs a Granada Television documentary, "Living With Michael Jackson", an intimate behind-the scenes-look at the star's day-to-day life at Neverland, including extensive interview segments conducted by journalist, Martin Bashir. Filmed over eight months between May the previous year and January 2003, it will broadcast on February 6–8 on ABC in the United States. The revealing exposé includes a baffling denial that he has undergone plastic surgery on his face, a shopping spree in Las Vegas when he spends $6 million in one store and a frank and naive admission that he allows boys to sleep with him in his bedroom confirming that "many children" have shared his bed—in a non-sexual manner. The program causes intense media speculation and controversy—and prompts a complaint of child molestation from the mother of a future accuser. Jackson's camp will immediately release his own version of the interview—filmed by Hamid Moslehi—called "Take Two: The Footage You Were Never Meant To See" in a hasty effort at damage control.

Der britische Fernsehsender ITV strahlt den Dokumentarfilm „Living with Michael Jackson" von Granada Television aus, ein Blick hinter die Kulissen auf den privaten Alltag in Neverland mit Ausschnitten aus einem Interview, das der Journalist Martin Bashir mit Jackson führte. Die zwischen Mai 2002 und Januar 2003 gedrehte Enthüllungsstory enthält unter anderem Jacksons verblüffende Leugnung, sich jemals plastischer Gesichtschirurgie unterzogen zu haben, ferner einen Einkaufsbummel in Las Vegas, bei dem Jackson in einem Geschäft sechs Millionen Dollar ausgibt, sowie das ebenso freimütige wie naive Geständnis, dass er

Jungen erlaube, mit ihm in seinem Schlafzimmer zu schlafen, und dass „viele Kinder" bereits – auf nichtsexuelle Art und Weise – sein Bett mit ihm geteilt hätten. Die Sendung löst heftige Spekulationen und kontroverse Diskussionen in den Medien und eine weitere Anzeige wegen Kindesmissbrauchs aus. Jacksons Lager versucht, den Schaden zu begrenzen, und veröffentlicht unter dem Titel: „Take Two: The Footage You Were Never Meant to See" („Take 2: Das Material, das Sie nie zu sehen bekommen sollten") seine eigene Version des Interviews, gedreht von Hamid Moslehi.

La chaîne de télévision britannique ITV diffuse un documentaire produit par Granada Television intitulé « Living With Michael Jackson », une incursion dans la vie quotidienne de la star à Neverland, ponctuée d'extraits d'un entretien entre Jackson et le journaliste Martin Bashir. Tourné sur plus de huit mois entre mai 2002 et janvier 2003, il passera également sur la chaîne américaine ABC les 6 et 8 février. Dans ce film riche en révélations, il nie encore avoir subi des opérations de chirurgie esthétique au visage ou avoir dépensé six millions de dollars d'un coup, et dans une seule boutique, à Las Vegas. Il admet aussi, avec une franchise et une naïveté déconcertantes, qu'il permet à de jeunes garçons de dormir dans sa chambre et confirme que « de nombreux enfants » ont partagé sa couche, mais pas de façon sexuelle. Le documentaire déclenche à nouveau spéculations et scandale, et la mère d'un enfant invité chez la star porte plainte pour abus sexuels sur mineur. L'entourage de Jackson diffuse immédiatement sa version de l'interview intitulée « Deuxième prise : les images que vous ne deviez pas voir ».

WEDNESDAY, JUNE 11, 2003

Returning to his Gary birthplace, Jackson greets students at Roosevelt High School, as he makes his first public appearance in the town in over 20 years.

Jackson kehrt in seine Heimatstadt Gary zurück, wo er bei seinem ersten öffentlichen Auftritt in der Stadt seit über 20 Jahren Schüler der Roosevelt High School begrüßt.

De retour dans sa ville natale de Gary pour la première fois depuis vingt ans, il vient saluer les élèves du lycée Roosevelt.

TUESDAY, JUNE 24, 2003

Being honored with the Lifetime Achievement Award at the annual BET Awards, James Brown is caught by surprise when an unannounced Jackson comes onstage at the end of his act and places Brown's trademark cape around his shoulders. As the music continues, Jackson demonstrates some moves learnt from the Godfather of Soul.

Während James Brown bei der jährlichen Verleihung der BET Awards die Auszeichnung für sein Lebenswerk entgegennimmt, wird er von einem unangekündigten Auftritt Jacksons überrascht, der Browns typisches Cape um seine Schultern legt. Während die Musik weiterspielt, zeigt Jackson einige der Schritte, die er vom „Godfather of Soul" gelernt hat.

James Brown vient de recevoir un BET Award couronnant l'ensemble de sa carrière et se trouve tout surpris de voir Jackson monter sur la scène et placer sur ses épaules sa cape fétiche de patriarche. La musique reprend et Jackson ébauche quelques mouvements de danse qu'il a appris du Parrain de la Soul.

SATURDAY, AUGUST 30, 2003
Celebrating his 45th birthday, Jackson sits in the audience at the "Michael Jackson—A Celebration of Love" concert, attended by fans from around the world, at the Orpheum Theater in Los Angeles.

Zur Feier seines 45. Geburtstags sitzt Jackson bei dem Konzert „Michael Jackson – A Celebration of Love" im Orpheum Theater von Los Angeles, das von Fans aus aller Welt besucht wird, im Publikum.

Pour son 45ᵉ anniversaire, Jackson assiste en spectateur au concert « Michael Jackson – A Celebration of Love », parmi des fans venus du monde entier, à l'Orpheum Theater de Los Angeles.

"Over the years we became a family. You are all my family. My children are your children and all children of the world are our children and our responsibility."

„Im Laufe der Jahre sind wir zu einer Familie geworden. Ihr seid alle meine Familie. Meine Kinder sind eure Kinder, und alle Kinder der Welt sind unsere Kinder und unsere Verantwortung."

« Au fil des années, nous sommes devenus une famille. Vous faites tous partie de ma famille. Mes enfants sont vos enfants et tous les enfants du monde sont nos enfants, nous en sommes responsables. »

MICHAEL JACKSON, AUGUST 30, 2003

Santa Barbara County Sheriff's Dept.

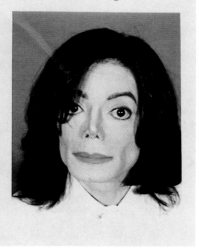

11/20/2003
Photo Image of:
NAME: JACKSON, MICHAEL
RAC: B   SEX: M
DOB: 8/29/1958   AGE: 45
HGT: 511   WGT: 120
BLD: CMP:
HAI: BLK   EYE: BRO
MKS:
BOOKING #:   621785

THURSDAY, NOVEMBER 20, 2003

Two days after 70 investigators from the Santa Barbara County District Attorney's Office and Sheriff's Department arrive at the Neverland Ranch with a search warrant, Jackson hands himself over to California police, charged with "lewd or lascivious acts" with a child younger than 14 under section 288(a) of the California Penal Code. The case has been investigated following allegations by the mother of 13-year-old cancer victim Gavin Arvizo, who alleges that Jackson "committed a lewd and lascivious act upon, and with, the boy's body and certain parts and members thereof, with the intent of arousing, appealing to and gratifying the lust, passions and sexual desires" of the defendant. Among many personal items removed from Neverland are pornography, syringes, the powerful painkiller Demerol and other prescription drugs. Jackson posts $3 million bail and vehemently denies any wrongdoing.

Zwei Tage nachdem siebzig Ermittler der Staatsanwaltschaft und des Sheriffsbüros des Bezirks Santa Barbara die Neverland-Ranch durchsucht haben, stellt sich Jackson der Polizei. Er wird „lüsterner oder unzüchtiger Handlungen" mit einem Kind, das jünger ist als 14 Jahre, bezichtigt. Die Ermittlungen wurden aufgenommen, nachdem die Mutter des dreizehnjährigen krebskranken Gavin Arvizo Anzeige erstattet hatte, weil Jackson „eine lüsterne und unzüchtige Handlung an und mit dem Körper des Jungen und bestimmten

Teilen und Gliedern seines Körpers" vorgenommen habe „mit der Absicht, die Lust, Leidenschaft und sexuellen Wünsche des Beschuldigten zu erregen, zu reizen und zu befriedigen". Zu den persönlichen Gegenständen, die aus Neverland entfernt werden, gehören pornografische Erzeugnisse, Spritzen, das Analgetikum Pethidin und andere verschreibungspflichtige Medikamente. Jackson hinterlegt drei Millionen Dollar Kaution und streitet jegliches Fehlverhalten vehement ab.

Deux jours après que 70 enquêteurs des bureaux du procureur et du shérif du comté de Santa Barbara se sont présentés à Neverland avec un mandat de perquisition, Jackson se rend à la police californienne. Il est inculpé pour «actes obscènes ou lascifs» sur un mineur de moins de 14 ans. L'enquête a été menée à partir des allégations de Janet Arvizo, la mère de Gavin Arvizo, un garçon cancéreux de 13 ans, qui affirme que Jackson, selon les termes légaux officiels, a «commis volontairement et illégalement un acte obscène et lascif sur le corps et certaines parties du corps d'un enfant âgé de moins de 14 ans, dans l'intention d'assouvir ses pulsions et ses désirs sexuels». Parmi les objets personnels confisqués par la police à Neverland figurent des magazines pornographiques, des seringues, des flacons de Demerol et d'autres médicaments délivrés sur ordonnance. Jackson verse une caution de trois millions de dollars et ressort libre.

SUNDAY, DECEMBER 28, 2003

Five days after he is formally charged with four counts of lewd conduct with a child younger than 14; one count of attempted lewd conduct; four counts of administering alcohol to facilitate child molestation; and one count of conspiracy to commit child abduction, false imprisonment or extortion, Jackson is interviewed by Ed Bradley on CBS-TV's "60 Minutes."

Fünf Tage nachdem Jackson formell des unzüchtigen Verhaltens mit einem Kind unter 14 Jahren in vier Fällen, eines Versuchs unzüchtigen Verhaltens, der Verabreichung von Alkohol zur Erleichterung des Kindesmissbrauchs in vier Fällen und in einem Fall der

Anstiftung zur Kindesentführung, zur unberechtigten Inhaftierung oder zur Erpressung beschuldigt wurde, wird er im Nachrichtenmagazin „60 Minutes" des Fernsehsenders CBS von Ed Bradley interviewt.

Cinq jours après avoir été officiellement accusé de tentative d'enlèvement d'enfant, tentative de séquestration et tentative d'extorsion (chef d'accusation 1), d'abus sexuel sur mineur (chefs 2, 3, 4, 5), de tentative d'abus sexuel sur mineur (chef 6) et d'administration d'alcool à un mineur dans le but de commettre un crime sur lui (chefs 7, 8 9 et 10), Jackson est interviewé par Ed Bradley sur CBS pour l'émission «60 Minutes».

"Before I would hurt a child, I would slit my wrists. I would never hurt a child. It's totally false. I was outraged. I could never do something like that."

„Bevor ich einem Kind etwas antun würde, würde ich mir die Pulsadern aufschlitzen. Ich würde nie ein Kind verletzen. Es ist völlig falsch. Ich war entsetzt. Ich könnte so etwas nie tun."

«Je me trancherais les veines plutôt que de faire du mal à un enfant. Je ne ferais jamais de mal à un enfant. Tout cela est faux. J'ai été très choqué. Je ne pourrais jamais faire une chose pareille.»

MICHAEL JACKSON

FRIDAY, JANUARY 16, 2004

Jackson is arraigned at the Santa Maria, California courthouse and rebuked by Judge Melville for showing up 20 minutes late. He will be indicted on April 24.

Jackson wird im Gerichtsgebäude von Santa Maria, Kalifornien, zu den Anschuldigungen vernommen und von Richter Melville gerügt, weil er 20 Minuten zu spät erscheint. Jackson wird am 24. April offiziell angeklagt.

Jackson comparaît devant la Cour de justice de Californie à Santa Maria et se voit réprimandé par le juge Melville pour s'être présenté avec 20 minutes de retard. Il sera officiellement inculpé le 24 avril.

WEDNESDAY, MARCH 31, 2004

Jackson goes to Washington's Capitol Hill and meets with Democratic Representative Sheila Jackson Lee and African-American lawmakers to offer his support on the fight against AIDS and help for African children.

Jackson trifft sich auf dem Capitol Hill in Washington mit der Abgeordneten Sheila Jackson Lee von der Demokratischen Partei sowie mit Parlamentariern afrikanischer Abstammung, um seine Unterstützung für den Kampf gegen Aids und die Hilfe für afrikanische Kinder anzubieten.

Jackson se rend au Capitole, à Washington, pour rencontrer la députée démocrate Sheila Jackson Lee et d'autres représentants afro-américains, auxquels il propose son aide dans la lutte contre le sida et l'assistance aux enfants africains.

THURSDAY, APRIL 1, 2004

Jackson receives the Golden Elephant Humanitarian Award from the African Ambassadors' Spouses Association after a group of children perform for him at the Ethiopian Embassy in Washington.

Jackson erhält den „Golden Elephant Humanitarian Award" von der African Ambassadors' Spouses Association, nachdem eine Kindergruppe für ihn in der äthiopischen Botschaft in Washington aufgetreten ist.

Jackson reçoit le Golden Elephant Humanitarian Award de l'Association des épouses d'ambassadeurs africains à l'issue d'un spectacle au cours duquel des enfants chantent pour lui à l'ambassade d'Éthiopie à Washington.

MONDAY, FEBRUARY 28, 2005

Opening statements begin in the Superior Court of the State of California, "held in and for the County of Santa Barbara" for The People of the State of California v. Michael Joseph Jackson. The media circus which has fed off every detail leading up to the trial reaches fever pitch with the world's media permanently camped outside the courtroom for 15 weeks, alongside a throng of devoted fans. Jackson—looking frail and weak throughout the ordeal—is frequently late for court sessions. As the case proceeds Judge Melville allows prosecution evidence regarding five other boys who were alleged to have been involved in sexual behavior with the star; the prosecution also submits a collection of some 70 pornographic magazines found at Neverland by the police during its material search of his home. Jackson will not testify during the case. His accuser will, claiming in graphic detail, allegations of molestation by Jackson on two separate occasions in early 2003.

Vor einem übergeordneten Gericht des Staates Kalifornien „im und für den Bezirk Santa Barbara" werden die Eröffnungsplädoyers im Strafverfahren „Volk des Staates Kalifornien gegen Michael Joseph Jackson" gehalten. Der Medienzirkus, der vor Beginn der Verhandlung begierig jede Einzelheit aufgeschnappt und verbreitet hat, erlebt nun seinen Höhepunkt, als Medienvertreter aus aller Welt ununterbrochen 15 Wochen lang – neben einem Heer treuer Fans – vor dem Gerichtsgebäude Stellung beziehen. Jackson, der während der Tortur schwach und gebrechlich wirkt, erscheint häufig mit Verspätung zur Verhandlung, in deren Verlauf Richter Melville der Anklage gestattet, Beweise zu weiteren Fällen einzubringen, in denen der Beschuldigte an sexuellen Handlungen mit fünf Jungen beteiligt gewesen sein soll. Die Anklagevertretung legt zudem eine Sammlung von rund siebzig pornografischen Zeitschriften vor, die während der polizeilichen Hausdurchsuchung auf Neverland gefunden wurden. Jackson wird während der Verhandlung nicht aussagen. Sein Ankläger hingegen schildert in allen Einzelheiten die angebliche Belästigung durch Jackson bei zwei verschiedenen Gelegenheiten Anfang 2003.

Début des débats devant la Cour supérieure de justice de Californie. Le cirque médiatique, qui s'alimente depuis des mois déjà des moindres détails concernant le procès, tourne à la fièvre mondiale : des centaines de journalistes campent devant le tribunal pendant 15 semaines, aux côtés d'un noyau dur de fans toujours fervents. Jackson, silhouette frêle écrasée par l'épreuve, arrive fréquemment en retard aux audiences. À mesure que les débats progressent, le juge Melville permet à l'accusation de présenter des preuves concernant cinq autres victimes présumées, cinq jeunes garçons qui auraient avoir subi les assauts sexuels de la star. Le procureur soumet aussi à la Cour une collection de quelque 70 magazines pornographiques trouvés par la police lors de la fouille de Neverland. Jackson n'est pas appelé à la barre des témoins. Son accusateur, en revanche, raconte avec force détails de quelle manière Jackson aurait abusé de lui à deux reprises, début 2003.

MONDAY, JUNE 13, 2005

574 days after the beginning of the investigation and after 32 hours of deliberation over seven days, the eight-woman, four-man jury finds Jackson not guilty on all charges. Accompanied by family members as he walks outside the courtroom, he is expressionless and makes no statement. Suffering increasing weight-loss and stress, it is reported that Jackson has become addicted to morphine and Demerol. Never returning to Neverland, Jackson will shortly relocate to Bahrain at the invitation of Sheikh Abdullah.

574 Tage nach Beginn der Ermittlungen und nach 32 Stunden Beratung über einen Zeitraum von sieben Tagen befinden die acht weiblichen und vier männlichen Geschworenen Jackson in allen Anklagepunkten für unschuldig. Er ist ausdruckslos und äußert sich nicht, als er in Begleitung von Angehörigen aus dem Gerichtsgebäude tritt. Es wird berichtet, dass Jackson, der immer mehr unter Gewichtsverlust und psychischer Belastung leidet, inzwischen süchtig nach Morphin und Pethidin sei. Er wird nie nach Neverland zurückkehren und zieht kurze Zeit später auf Einladung Scheich Abdullahs nach Bahrain.

Après 574 jours d'enquête et 32 heures de délibération sur sept jours, le jury composé de huit femmes et quatre hommes juge Jackson non coupable de l'ensemble des charges retenues contre lui. Lorsqu'il quitte le tribunal, entouré de membres de sa famille, il ne manifeste aucune émotion et ne fait aucune déclaration. Jackson, très stressé et amaigri, souffrirait d'une addiction à la morphine et au Demerol. Il ne retournera jamais à Neverland, et s'installe un temps à Bahreïn, sur l'invitation du cheikh Abdullah.

WEDNESDAY, NOVEMBER 15, 2006

A virtual recluse since his court case the previous year, Jackson appears at the World Music Awards in London to receive the Diamond Award for selling over 100 million albums. During his trip to the capital he also visits the Guinness World Records office in London where he is presented with eight records including "Most Successful Entertainer of All Time" and "First Entertainer to Earn More Than 100 Million Dollars in a Year."

Jackson, der sich seit der Gerichtsverhandlung im Vorjahr praktisch völlig aus der Öffentlichkeit zurückgezogen hat, erscheint bei der Verleihung der World Music Awards in London, um den „Diamond Award" für den Verkauf von über 100 Millionen Alben entgegenzunehmen. Während seines Aufenthalts in London besucht er auch das Büro von Guinness World Records, wo er mit acht Rekorden ausgezeichnet wird, darunter die Rekorde als „Erfolgreichster Entertainer aller Zeiten" und „Erster Entertainer, der in einem Jahr mehr als 100 Millionen Dollar verdient hat".

Alors qu'il vit en reclus depuis la fin de son procès, Jackson fait une apparition aux World Music Awards, à Londres, pour recevoir le Diamond Award, qui couronne plus de 100 millions d'albums vendus. Pendant son séjour, il se rend aussi au siège des Records du Monde Guinness, où il se voit remettre huit attestations, notamment de « Plus grand homme de scène de tous les temps » et de « Premier homme de scène à avoir gagné plus de 100 millions de dollars en une année ».

SATURDAY, DECEMBER 30, 2006

Jackson pays his respects to the Godfather of Soul, James Brown, at the James Brown Arena in Augusta, Georgia. Brown, a major influence on Jackson, passed away on Christmas Day.

Jackson erweist dem am Weihnachtstag verstorbenen „Godfather of Soul" James Brown in der James Brown Arena in Augusta, Georgia, die letzte Ehre.

Jackson rend hommage au Parrain de la Soul, James Brown, à la James Brown Arena d'Augusta (Georgie). Brown, influence majeure de Jackson, est mort le jour de Noël.

WEDNESDAY, MARCH 7, 2007

During a visit to Tokyo to attend a fan appreciation dinner in his honor (for 400 people paying 400,000 yen ($3,500)/plate) Jackson makes the following statement to an Associated Press journalist: "I've been in the entertainment industry since I was 6 years old. As Charles Dickens says, 'It's been the best of times, the worst of times.' But I would not change my career. While some have made deliberate attempts to hurt me, I take it in stride because I have a loving family, a strong faith and wonderful friends and fans who have, and continue, to support me." It is widely reported that Jackson's worsening financial plight—first revealed during his 2005 court case—is becoming critical. A $270 million loan from the Bank of America has been recently refinanced by Fortress Investments using Jackson's already highly-leveraged publishing company partnership with Sony as collateral.

Während Jackson sich in Tokio aufhält, um an einem Abendessen teilzunehmen, das Fans zu seinen Ehren ausrichten (für 400 Personen, die jeweils 400.000 Yen [ca. 3.000 Euro] pro Gedeck zahlen mussten), erklärt Jackson gegenüber einem Journalisten der Associated Press: „Ich bin seit meinem sechsten Lebensjahr in der Unterhaltungsindustrie tätig. Wie Charles Dickens sagt: ‚Es war die beste aller Zeiten, es war die schlimmste aller Zeiten'. Aber ich würde meine Karriere nicht ändern wollen. Obwohl einige absichtlich versuchten, mich zu verletzen, kann ich ganz locker damit umgehen, weil ich eine liebende Familie habe, einen starken Glauben und wunderbare Freunde und Fans, die mich unterstützt haben und es noch immer tun." Es wird vielfach berichtet, dass Jacksons zunehmende finanzielle Probleme einen kritischen Punkt erreicht haben. Ein Kredit der Bank of America über 270 Millionen Dollar wurde kurz zuvor von Fortress Investments refinanziert.

De passage à Tokyo pour participer à un dîner donné en son honneur par une association de fans locaux (400 invités qui ont déboursé 400 000 yens, soit plus de 3 000 euros chacun), Jackson fait la déclaration suivante à un journaliste de l'agence Associated Press : « Je suis dans l'industrie du spectacle depuis que j'ai 6 ans... j'ai vécu le meilleur et le pire. Mais je ne changerais rien à ma carrière. Alors que certains ont délibérément tenté de me faire du mal, je prends les choses avec calme, parce que j'ai une famille qui m'aime, une foi sincère et des amis et des fans merveilleux... » Il semble que les problèmes financiers de Jackson atteignent un point critique. Il parvient à éviter la faillite en négociant le refinancement d'un emprunt de 270 millions de dollars, et utilise comme garantie son précieux catalogue musical (déjà fortement grevé) et son partenariat avec Sony.

FRIDAY, FEBRUARY 8, 2008

With an international rollout following over the next three days, **Thriller 25** is released by SonyBMG in Australia marking the 25th anniversary of the release of the world's best-selling album. The reissue includes the original tracks, new remixes featuring guest vocalists Akon, will.i.am, Fergie and Kanye West, other bonus material and a DVD. It will sell three million copies worldwide in 12 weeks.

Vor der internationalen Kampagne, die in den nächsten drei Tagen folgen wird, bringt SonyBMG zur Feier des 25. Jahrestags der Veröffentlichung des meistverkauften Plattenalbums der Welt in Australien **Thriller 25** auf den Markt. Die Neuauflage enthält sowohl die Originaltracks als auch Remix-Versionen mit den Gastinterpreten Akon, will.i.am, Fergie und Kanye West, weiteres Bonusmaterial und eine DVD. In zwölf Wochen werden weltweit drei Millionen Exemplare verkauft.

SonyBMG inaugure trois jours de promotion intensive autour du 25ᵉ anniversaire de l'album le plus vendu au monde en sortant en Australie l'album commémoratif (et éminemment commercial) **Thriller 25**, qui comprend, outre les titres originaux, de nouvelles versions signées Akon, will.i.am, Fergie et Kanye West, d'autres bonus, et un DVD. En 12 semaines, il se vend à trois millions d'exemplaires dans le monde.

MONDAY, FEBRUARY 25, 2008

With its owner having not lived there since his 2005 trial, Jackson is informed by the Financial Title Company that unless he pays off $24,525,906.61 within three weeks, a public auction will be held of the land, its buildings, and all other items on the Neverland estate. A foreclosure auction scheduled for May 12 will be forestalled when Colony Capital LLC purchases the loan.

Jackson, der seit dem Prozess von 2005 nicht mehr auf Neverland gelebt hat, erfährt von der Financial Title Company, dass das Grundstück selbst, die Gebäude und alles andere, was sich auf dem Grundstück befindet, öffentlich versteigert werden wird, sofern er nicht innerhalb von drei Wochen seine Schulden in Höhe von 24.525.906,61 Dollar begleicht. Eine für den 12. Mai angesetzte Zwangsversteigerung wird dadurch verhindert, dass die Colony Capital LLC den Kredit aufkauft.

La Financial Title Company informe Jackson qu'à moins qu'il verse 24 525 906,61 dollars dans un délai de trois semaines, les terres, bâtiments et tous les biens mobiliers et immobiliers composant la propriété de Neverland seront vendus aux enchères. La vente des biens saisis, fixée au 12 mai, est annulée lorsque le groupe d'investissement Colony Capital LLC rachète à Jackson son titre de propriété.

THURSDAY, MARCH 5, 2009

At the O2 Arena in London, Jackson re-emerges to personally announce "my final show performances in London. When I say this is it, it really means this is it. This is my final curtain call." Initially planned as a 10-date engagement, public interest in the "This Is It" event quickly inflates the number to a mammoth 50-concert residency—to be staged at the O2—and scheduled to begin on July 8, closing on March 6, 2010. The entire 1,150,000 tickets will sell out within hours when they go on sale the following week. Last month Jackson passed a strenuous five-hour physical required by the insurers of the planned concerts. On May 20, it is announced that the first concert has been pushed back to July 13 with three others being rescheduled.

In der O2 Arena in London taucht Jackson persönlich auf, um „meine letzten Showauftritte in London" anzukündigen. „Wenn ich sage, das war's, dann bedeutet das wirklich: Das war's. Dies ist mein letzter Vorhang." Die Veranstaltung „This Is It", die ursprünglich als eine Reihe von zehn Konzerten geplant war, steigert sich aufgrund des öffentlichen Interesses rasch zu einem Mammutprogramm von fünfzig Konzerten in der O2 Arena zwischen dem 8. Juli 2009 und dem 6. März

2010. Sämtliche 1.150.000 Eintrittskarten sind innerhalb weniger Stunden ausverkauft, als sie in der kommenden Woche in den Verkauf gehen. Im Februar hatte sich Jackson einem strapaziösen fünfstündigen Fitnesstest unterzogen, den die Versicherungsgesellschaft verlangt hatte. Am 20. Mai wird bekannt gegeben, dass das erste Konzert auf den 13. Juli verschoben wird und drei weitere Konzerttermine geändert werden.

Jackson ressort de l'ombre à l'O2 Arena de Londres, pour annoncer en personne ses «dernières représentations publiques à Londres. Quand je dis qu'ensuite c'est terminé, je veux vraiment dire terminé. Ce sera mon dernier lever de rideau». Cette ultime série de concerts ne doit au départ compter que 10 dates, mais l'engouement du public pour «This Is It» est tel que les organisateurs en programment finalement cinquante à l'O2 Arena, entre le 8 juillet et le 6 mars 2010. La semaine suivante, l'ensemble des 1 150 000 tickets s'arrache en quelques heures. En février, Jackson a subi cinq heures d'examens physiques et de tests d'effort, une mesure exigée par les assureurs de l'événement. Le 20 mai, les organisateurs annoncent que la date du premier concert est repoussée au 13 juillet.

WEDNESDAY, JUNE 24, 2009

At 9:30 pm Jackson begins three hours of rehearsals as part of ongoing preparations for his upcoming London concerts at the Staples Center in Los Angeles. AEG Live President Randy Phillips is in attendance, reporting to the Associated Press that "He was dancing as well or better than the 20-year-old dancers we surrounded him with. He looked great."

Um 21:30 Uhr beginnt Jackson im Staples Center in Los Angeles mit einer dreistündigen Probe im Rahmen seiner Vorbereitungen für die bevorstehenden Londoner Konzerte. Anwesend ist auch Randy Phillips, der Geschäftsführer des Konzertveranstalters AEG Live,

der gegenüber der Nachrichtenagentur Associated Press erklärt: „Er tanzte genauso gut oder besser als die zwanzigjährigen Tänzer, mit denen wir ihn umgaben. Er sah großartig aus."

À 21 h 30, Jackson entame trois heures de répétition au Staples Center de Los Angeles pour la préparation de ses prochains concerts londoniens. Le président d'AEG Live, Randy Phillips, est dans la salle. Il déclarera à l'Associated Press que Jackson «dansait aussi bien si ce n'est mieux que les danseurs de 20 ans qui l'entouraient. Il avait l'air en pleine forme».

THURSDAY, JUNE 25, 2009

At a mansion the star is renting on North Carolwood Drive in the Holby Hills area of Los Angeles, Jackson goes into cardiac arrest following the intravenous administration of the anaesthetic Propofol by his physician, Dr. Conrad Murray. The local Fire Department receives a 911 call from an unnamed male at 12:21 Pacific Coast Time, their paramedics arriving nine minutes later. Efforts at resuscitation are attempted en route to the UCLA Medical Center, and for a further 60 minutes at the hospital. He is officially pronounced dead, at 2:26 pm. His body is transported across town to the County Coroner's Office for an autopsy. Worldwide shock among his fans and celebrity friends is immediate and wall-to-wall media coverage erupts, lasting for several days. Internet traffic—described by Google as "volcanic"—causes social networking sites like Twitter to crash while the **Los Angeles Times** website—the first news organization to confirm Jackson's death—also suffers outages.

Jackson bricht nach einem Herzstillstand in einer von ihm gemieteten Villa am North Carolwood Drive im Bezirk Holby Hills in Los Angeles zusammen, nachdem sein Leibarzt, Dr. Conrad Murray, ihm das Narkosemittel Propofol verabreicht hatte. Die Feuerwehr von Los Angeles erhält um 12:21 Uhr einen Notruf von einer unbekannten männlichen Person, und die Rettungssanitäter treffen neun Minuten später ein. Wiederbelebungsmaßnahmen werden auf dem Weg in das UCLA Medical Center und weitere 60 Minuten lang im Krankenhaus selbst durchgeführt. Um 14:26 Uhr wird er offiziell für tot erklärt. Sein Leichnam wird zur

Obduktion zum Amt für Gerichtsmedizin des Bezirks Los Angeles gebracht. Fans und befreundete Prominente in aller Welt sind schockiert, und die Berichterstattung der Medien rund um die Uhr hält mehrere Tage an. Der Traffic im Internet, den Google als „vulkanisch" beschreibt, sorgt dafür, dass die Websites sozialer Netzwerke wie Twitter zusammenbrechen und die Website der **Los Angeles Times**, die als Erste Jacksons Tod bestätigte, zeitweise ausfällt.

Jackson fait un arrêt cardiaque dans la maison que loue la star sur North Carolwood Drive, dans les collines de Holby Hills après que son médecin personnel, le Dr Conrad Murray lui a administré du Propofol, un antalgique. À 12 h 21, les pompiers de Los Angeles reçoivent un appel d'un homme qui ne donne pas son identité. Neuf minutes plus tard, l'équipe d'intervention d'urgence arrive sur les lieux, tente de réanimer Jackson, en arrêt respiratoire, et continue ses efforts dans l'ambulance qui le conduit au Ronald Reagan UCLA Medical Center, puis à l'hôpital, pendant encore une heure. Son décès est prononcé à 14 h 26. Son corps est transporté aux bureaux de médecine légale du comté de Los Angeles pour autopsie. Le choc de cette annonce déferle sur les fans et les amis célèbres de Michael Jackson comme un raz-de-marée et la presse entre en ébullition pendant plusieurs jours. L'explosion des connexions sur Internet – que Google qualifie de «volcanique» – provoque la saturation des sites sociaux et d'information comme Twitter ou celui du **Los Angeles Times** (le premier organe de presse à confirmer la mort de Jackson).

FRIDAY, JUNE 26, 2009

Los Angeles Coroner's spokesman Craig Harvey confirms that Jackson was taking prescription medications, though comprehensive toxology reports will not be made available for at least six weeks. Brian Oxman, a former Jackson attorney and family friend, tells CNN: "I talked to his family about it, I warned them—I said that Michael is overmedicating and that I did not want to see this kind of a case develop." AEG's Randy Phillips confirms that Jackson had insisted on including Dr. Murray (who is reported by the AP to be in considerable financial debt) in his concert-preparation team (along with "Incredible Hulk" actor, Lou Ferrigno.) Quoting Jackson in his statement to the AP, Phillips says: "He just said, 'Look, this whole business revolves around me. I'm a machine and we have to keep the machine well-oiled,' and you don't argue with the King of Pop."

Craig Harvey, der Sprecher der Gerichtsmedizin von Los Angeles, bestätigt, dass Jackson verschreibungspflichtige Medikamente eingenommen hat, wenngleich ein umfassender toxikologischer Befund erst sechs Wochen später vorliegen werde. Brian Oxman, ein ehemaliger Rechtsanwalt von Michael Jackson und Freund der Familie, berichtet auf CNN: „Ich sprach mit seiner Familie darüber. Ich habe sie gewarnt. Ich sagte, dass Michael zu viele Medikamente zu sich nimmt und dass ich nicht zusehen wolle, wie sich diese Art von Fall weiterentwickelt." Randy Phillips, der Geschäftsführer von AEG Live, bestätigt, dass Jackson darauf bestanden habe, in sein Vorbereitungsteam für die geplanten Konzerte Dr. Murray aufzunehmen (der nach

Meldungen der Nachrichtenagentur AP in beträchtlichen finanziellen Schwierigkeiten steckt), ebenso wie Lou Ferrigno, der einst durch die Titelrolle in der Fernsehserie „The Incredible Hulk" bekannt wurde. In seiner Aussage gegenüber AP zitiert Phillips Jackson: „Er sagte nur: ‚Schaut mal, dieses ganze Geschäft dreht sich um mich. Ich bin eine Maschine, und wir müssen dafür sorgen, dass die Maschine gut geölt bleibt.' Und mit dem King of Pop diskutiert man nicht."

Le porte-parole du département de médecine légale de la police de Los Angeles Craig Harvey confirme que Jackson était sous traitement médical, même si les résultats toxicologiques précis ne seront pas disponibles avant au moins six semaines. Brian Oxman, ancien avocat de Jackson et ami de la famille, renchérit sur CNN : « J'en ai parlé à sa famille, je les ai prévenus – je leur ai dit que Michael prenait trop de médicaments et que je ne voulais pas que les choses empirent. » Le président d'AEG Live, Randy Phillips, confirme que Jackson a insisté pour intégrer le Dr Murray (qui serait lui-même considérablement endetté, selon l'AP) dans son équipe de préparation des concerts (tout comme l'interprète de l'« Incroyable Hulk », Lou Ferrigno). Il cite Jackson : « Il a juste dit : "Écoutez, tout ce business tourne autour de moi. Je suis une machine et il faut que la machine reste bien huilée", et on ne discute pas avec le Roi de la Pop. »

TUESDAY, JULY 7, 2009

After 12 days of unremitting media coverage—which has turned Jackson's death into a relentless public spectacle (described by Congressman Peter King as an "orgy of glorification")—the Michael Jackson Public Memorial Service takes place at the Staples Center in Los Angeles immediately following a private memorial at Forest Lawn cemetery attended by family members and 100 invited guests. Beamed live around the world and staged by concert promoter AEG Live—which received 1.6 million applications for the 17,500 free tickets—Jackson's golden casket is on display during the service in front of the Jackson family. Aural tributes are offered by Mariah Carey (*I'll Be There*) with Trey Lorenz, Lionel Richie (*Jesus Is Love*), Stevie Wonder (*Never Dreamed You'd Leave In Summer*), Jennifer Hudson (*Will You Be There*), John Mayer (*Human Nature*), Jermaine Jackson (*Smile*), Usher (*Gone Too Soon*), Shaheen Jafargholi (*Who's Lovin' You*), Andre Crouch Choir (*Soon And Very Soon*) and celebrity-filled renditions of *We Are The World* and *Heal The World*. Eulogies are given by the Reverend Al Sharpton, Brooke Shields, Queen Latifah, Magic Johnson, Kobe Bryant, Martin Luther King III, Ron Boyd, Pastor Lucious Smith, Bernice King, Congresswoman Sheila Jackson Lee, Smokey Robinson and Berry Gordy. The least-rehearsed moment is perhaps its most poignant, the event-closing, tear-filled words of Jackson's daughter Paris: "Ever since I was born, daddy has been the best father you could ever imagine—and I just wanted to say I love him so much."

Nach zwölf Tagen lückenloser Berichterstattung – durch die Jacksons Tod in ein unerbittliches Medienspektakel verwandelt wurde (der Abgeordnete Peter King sprach von einer „Orgie der Glorifizierung") – findet Michael Jacksons offizielle Trauerfeier im Staples Center in Los Angeles unmittelbar nach einer privaten Trauerfeier auf dem Forest Lawn Cemetery im Kreise der Familie und hundert geladener Gäste statt. Die offizielle Trauerfeier wird weltweit live übertragen und vom Konzertveranstalter AEG Live veranstaltet, der für die 17.500 kostenlosen Eintrittskarten 1,6 Millionen Bewerbungen erhalten hat. Jacksons vergoldeter Sarg wird während der Trauerfeier vor der Jackson-Familie aufgebahrt. Mariah Carey und Trey Lorenz (*I'll Be There*), Lionel Richie (*Jesus Is Love*), Stevie Wonder (*Never Dreamed You'd Leave In Summer*), Jennifer Hudson (*Will You Be There*), John Mayer (*Human Nature*), Jermaine Jackson (*Smile*), Usher (*Gone Too Soon*), Shaheen Jagarkholi (*Who's Lovin' You*) und der Andrae Crouch Choir (*Soon And Very Soon*) tragen musikalische Darbietungen vor, und unter Mitwirkung zahlreicher prominenter Künstler werden *We Are The World* und *Heal The World* zu Gehör gebracht. Wortbeiträge stammen von Reverend Al Sharpton, Brooke Shields, Queen Latifah, Magic Johnson, Kobe Bryant, Martin Luther King III, Ron Boyd, Pastor Lucious Smith, Bernice King, von der Abgeordneten Sheila Jackson Lee, von Smokey Robinson und Berry Gordy. Der spontanste Moment der Trauerfeier ist vielleicht der anrührendste: Unter Tränen spricht Jacksons Tochter Paris die abschließenden Worte: „Seit ich geboren wurde, war Daddy der beste Vater, den man sich überhaupt vorstellen kann – und ich wollte einfach sagen, ich liebe ihn so sehr."

La cérémonie publique d'hommage à Michael Jackson se tient au Staples Center de Los Angeles, après 12 jours d'une couverture médiatique intense qui transforme sa mort en spectacle continu (un acharnement que le représentant américain Peter King décrit comme «une orgie de glorification»). Sa famille et une centaine d'amis intimes ont auparavant assisté au service funèbre organisé au cimetière de Forest Lawn. Diffusée en direct sur les chaînes de télévision du monde entier, la soirée a été mise sur pied par le promoteur de la tournée avortée de Jackson, AEG Live – qui a reçu 1,6 millions de demandes pour les 17 500 billets gratuits qu'il avait mis en jeu. La famille Jackson est là, autour du cercueil doré de la star défunte. Les vedettes se succèdent sur scène pour lui rendre hommage : Mariah Carey chante *I'll Be There* avec Trey Lorenz, Lionel Richie *Jesus Is Love*, Stevie Wonder *Never Dreamed You'd Leave In Summer*, Jennifer Hudson *Will You Be There*, John Mayer *Human Nature*, Jermaine Jackson *Smile*, Usher *Gone Too Soon*, Shaheen Jafargholi *Who's Lovin' You*, l'Andre Crouch Choir *Soon And Very Soon*. Une foule d'artistes se rassemble aussi pour entonner *We Are The World* et *Heal The World*. L'éloge funèbre est prononcé par le révérend Al Sharpton, avec les témoignages de Brooke Shields, Queen Latifah, Magic Johnson, Kobe Bryant, Martin Luther King III, Ron Boyd, Pastor Lucious Smith, Bernice King, la réprésentante Sheila Jackson Lee, Smokey Robinson et Berry Gordy. Le moment le plus poignant est sans doute aussi le moins répété. Pour clore la soirée, sa fille Paris prend la parole, la voix brouillée de larmes : «Depuis que je suis née, papa a été le meilleur père qu'on puisse imaginer – et je voulais juste dire... que je l'aime tellement.»

3

ESSENTIAL RECORDINGS

DIE WICHTIGSTEN ALBEN

PRINCIPAUX ENREGISTREMENTS

FOREVER, MICHAEL
(1975)
1 We're Almost There **2** Take Me Back **3** One Day In Your Life **4** Cinderella Stay Awhile **5** We've Got Forever **6** Just A Little Bit Of You **7** You Are There **8** Dapper Dan **9** Dear Michael **10** I'll Come Home To You

OFF THE WALL
(1979)
1 Don't Stop 'Til You Get Enough **2** Rock With You **3** Working Day And Night **4** Get On The Floor **5** Off The Wall **6** Girlfriend **7** She's Out Of My Life **8** I Can't Help It **9** It's The Falling In Love **10** Burn This Disco Out

THRILLER
(1982)
1 Wanna Be Startin' Somethin' **2** Baby Be Mine **3** The Girl Is Mine **4** Thriller **5** Beat It **6** Billie Jean **7** Human Nature **8** P.Y.T. (Pretty Young Thing) **9** The Lady In My Life

BAD
(1987)
1 Bad **2** The Way You Make Me Feel **3** Speed Demon **4** Liberian Girl **5** Just Good Friends **6** Another Part Of Me **7** Man In The Mirror **8** I Just Can't Stop Loving You **9** Dirty Diana **10** Smooth Criminal **11** Leave Me Alone

DANGEROUS
(1991)
1 Jam **2** Why You Wanna Trip On Me **3** In The Closet **4** She Drives Me Wild **5** Remember The Time **6** Can't Let Her Get Away **7** Heal The World **8** Black Or White **9** Who Is It **10** Give In To Me **11** Will You Be There **12** Keep The Faith **13** Gone Too Soon **14** Dangerous

INVINCIBLE
(2001)
1 Unbreakable **2** Heartbreaker **3** Invincible **4** Break Of Dawn **5** Heaven Can Wait **6** You Rock My World **7** Butterflies **8** Speechless **9** 2000 Watts **10** You Are My Life **11** Privacy **12** Don't Walk Away **13** Cry **14** The Lost Children **15** Whatever Happens **16** Threatened

4

AWARDS & CHART HISTORY

AUSZEICHNUNGEN & CHARTPLATZIERUNGEN

RÉCOMPENSES ET HISTORIQUE DES VENTES

UNITED STATES CERTIFICATIONS
UNITED STATES SINGLES

The Girl Is Mine – Gold / *I Just Can't Stop Loving You* – Gold / *Beat It* – Platinum / *Billie Jean* – Platinum / *Don't Stop 'Til You Get Enough* – Platinum / *Rock With You* – Platinum / *She's Out Of My Life* – Gold / *Thriller* – Platinum / *Black Or White* – Platinum / *In The Closet* – Gold / *Remember The Time* – Gold / *Say Say Say* – Platinum / *Will You Be There?* – Gold / *Scream* – Platinum / *You Are Not Alone* – Platinum / *Billie Jean* – Gold / *Don't Stop 'Til You Get Enough* – Gold / *Thriller* – Gold

UNITED STATES ALBUMS

Bad – 8 times Platinum / *Off The Wall* – 7 times Platinum / *HIStory* – Past Present And Future Book I – 7 times Platinum / *Blood On The Dance Floor* – History In The Mix – Platinum / *Dangerous* – 7 times Platinum / *Invincible* – 2 times Platinum / *Greatest Hits – History Volume 1 –* Gold / *Number Ones* – Platinum / *Thriller* – 27 times Platinum

UNITED KINGDOM CERTIFICATIONS
UNITED KINGDOM SINGLES

Ben – Silver / *Don't Stop Til You Get Enough* – Silver / *One Day In Your Life* – Gold / *Beat It* – Silver / *Billie Jean* – Gold / *Say, Say, Say –* Silver / *Farewell My Summer Love* – Gold / *Black Or White* – Silver / *Heal The World* – Gold / *Earth Song* – Platinum / *You Are Not Alone* – Gold / *They Don't Care About Us* – Silver / *Blood On The Dance Floor* – Gold

UNITED KINGDOM ALBUMS

Off The Wall – Platinum / *The Best Of Michael Jackson* – SIlver / *18 Greatest Hits* – Platinum / *Love Songs* – Platinum / *The Michael Jackson Mix* – Platinum / *Bad* – 13 times Platinum / *Thriller* – 11 times Platinum / *Dangerous* – 6 times Platinum / *HIStory* – 4 times Platinum / *Invincible* – Platinum / *Number Ones –* 4 times Platinum

MISCELLANEOUS AWARDS

Favorite Male Artist (Soul/R&B), Favorite Album (Soul/R&B), Favorite Single (Soul/R&B), Favorite Male Artist (Pop/Rock), Favorite Album (Pop/ Rock), Favorite Single (Pop/Rock), Favorite Video (Pop/ Rock), Favorite Video (Soul/R&B), Award of Merit, Award of Appreciation, Song of the Year, Award of Achievement, International Artist Award, Artist of the Century – American Music Awards – 1980, 1981, 1984, 1986, 1988, 1989, 1993, 1996, 2002 / 1st Michael Jackson Award of Achievement, BMI Urban Award, BMI Icon Award – BMI Urban Awards – 1990, 2003, 2008 / Good Scout Humanitarian Award – Boy Scouts of America – 1990 / Best International Solo Artist, Best British Album, Best International Artist (Male), Best Music Video, Artist of a Generation Award – BRIT Awards – 1984, 1988, 1989, 1996 / Artist of the Decade – British TV Industry Awards – 1989 / Outstanding Humanitarian Award – Bollywood Awards – 1999 / Magic Life Award – Celebrate the Magic Foundation – 2002 / Caring for Kids Award – Children's Choice Awards – 1994 / Best Video – Critic's Choice Awards – 1989 / Most Important Entertainer of the Decade – "Entertainment Tonight" – 1989 / No. 1 Entertainer of the Year – **Forbes Magazine** – 1988, 1989 / Doris Day Music Award – Genesis Awards – 1996 / Best Pop Song, Best Male Vocal Performance (R&B), Album of the Year, Record of the Year, Producer of the Year, Best R&B Song, Best Recording for Children (Narration), Best Male Vocal Performance (Pop), Best Male Vocal Performance (Rock), Best Long Form Video, Song of the Year, Record of the Year, Best Pop Performance (Duo/Group), Best Short Form Music Video, Living Legend Award – Grammy Awards – 1971, 1980, 1984, 1985, 1986, 1990, 1993, 1996 / Grammy Hall of Fame – *I Want You Back* (1999), *Thriller* (2008), *Off The Wall* (2008) / Humanitarian Award – Harry Chapin Memorial – 1995 / Hollywood Walk of Fame Star – 1984 / Best Male Artist of the Year, Best Male Performer – MTV European Music Awards – 1995 / Legend Award – MTV Japan Awards – 2006 / Best Overall Performance Video, Best Choreography, Viewer's Choice Award, Best Special Effects, Best Art Direction, Best Dance Video – MTV Video Music Awards – 1984, 1989, 1995 / Video Vanguard Award, the Greatest Video in the History of the World – MTV Video Vanguard Awards – 1988, 1989 / Artist of the Millennium Award – MTV Artist of the Millennium Award – 2002 / H. Claude Hodson Medal of Freedom, Best Male Artist, Best Album, Leonard Carter Humanitarian Award, 25th Anniversary Entertainer of the Year Award, Outstanding Music Video, Outstanding Performance Variety Series/Special – NAACP Image Awards – 1984, 1988, 1993, 2002 / Lifetime Achievement Award – National Association of Black Owned Broadcasters – 1992 / Power of Oneness Award – Oneness Awards – 2003 / Presidential Humanitarian Award, Artist of the Decade, Point of Light Ambassador – Presidential Awards – 1984, 1990, 1992 / Rock and Roll Hall of Fame – 1997, 2001 / Video of the Decade – **Rolling Stone** 1989 / Songwriter's Hall of Fame – 2002 / Best Male Singer of the Year, R&B Album of the Year, 1st annual Sammy Davis Jr./Heritage Award, Best R&B/Urban Contemporary (Male), Best R&B/Urban Contemporary (Music Video), Silver Award for 1980s Artist of the Decade, Humanitarian of the Year Award, Best R&B Album, Best Single (Male), Hall of Fame – Soul Train Awards – 1988, 1989, 1990, 1993, 1995 / Frederick D. Patterson Award, Doctor of Humane Letters – United Negro College Fund – 1988 / Special Commendation for Positive Role Models – United States Congress – 1972

US CHART HISTORY

US CHART SINGLES

Week of Entry	Highest Position	Wks	Title	Catalog Number
89 (October 30, 1971)	4 (December 11, 1971)	14	*Got To Be There*	Motown M-1191F
68 (March 11, 1972)	2 (April 22, 1972)	13	*Rockin' Robin*	Motown M-1197F
59 (May 27, 1972)	16 (July 15, 1972)	11	*I Wanna Be Where You Are*	Motown M-1202F
85 (August 5, 1972)	1 (October 14, 1972)	16	*Ben*	Motown M-1207F
84 (May 5, 1973)	50 (June 2, 1973)	7	*With A Child's Heart*	Motown M-1218F
89 (March 1, 1975)	54 (April 5, 1975)	8	*We're Almost There*	Motown M-1341F
90 (June 7, 1975)	23 (August 9, 1975)	12	*Just A Little Bit Of You*	Motown M-1349F
77 (September 9, 1978)	41 (October 21, 1978)	9	*Ease On Down The Road**	MCA MCA 40947
83 (February 24, 1979)	81 (March 3, 1979)	3	*You Can't Win (Part 1)*	Epic 8-50654
87 (July 28, 1979)	1 (October 13, 1979)	21	*Don't Stop Till You Get Enough*	Epic 1-65983
76 (November 3, 1979)	1 (January 19, 1980)	24	*Rock With You*	Epic 9-50797
53 (February 16, 1980)	10 (April 12, 1980)	17	*Off The Wall*	Epic 9-50838
57 (April 19, 1980)	10 (June 21, 1980)	16	*She's Out Of My Life*	Epic 9-50871
81 (April 18, 1981)	55 (May 16, 1981)	7	*One Day In Your Life*	Motown M-1512F
45 (November 6, 1982)	2 (January 8, 1983)	18	*The Girl Is Mine***	Epic 34-03288
47 (January 22, 1983)	1 (March 5, 1983)	24	*Billie Jean*	Epic 34-03509
78 (February 26, 1983)	1 (April 30, 1983)	25	*Beat It*	Epic 34-03759
41 (May 28, 1983)	5 (July 16, 1983)	15	*Wanna Be Startin' Somethin'*	Epic 34-03914
48 (July 23, 1983)	7 (September 17, 1983)	14	*Human Nature*	Epic 34-04026
75 (October 8, 1983)	10 (November 26, 1983)	16	*P. Y. T. (Pretty Young Thing)*	Epic 34-04165
26 (October 15, 1983)	1 (December 10, 1983)	22	*Say Say Say***	Columbia 38-04168
20 (February 11, 1984)	4 (March 3, 1984)	14	*Thriller*	Epic 34-04364
81 (May 26, 1984)	38 (June 30, 1984)	12	*Farewell My Summer Love*	Motown M-1739F
40 (September 19, 1987)	1 (October 24, 1987)	14	*Bad*	Epic 34-07418
37 (August 8, 1987)	1 (September 19, 1987)	14	*I Just Can't Stop Loving You****	Epic 34-07253
44 (November 21, 1987)	1 (January 23, 1988)	18	*The Way You Make Me Feel*	Epic 34-07645
48 (February 6, 1988)	1 (March 26, 1988)	17	*The Man In The Mirror*	Epic 34-0768
53 (May 7, 1988)	1 (July 2, 1988)	14	*Dirty Diana*	Epic 34-07739
89 (May 7, 1988)	80 (May 28, 1988)	6	*Get It****	Motown 193MF
54 (July 23, 1988)	11 (September 10, 1988)	13	*Another Part Of Me*	Epic 34-07962
66 (November 12, 1988)	7 (January 14, 1989)	15	*Smooth Criminal*	Epic 34-08044
35 (November 23, 1991)	1 (December 7, 1991)	20	*Black Or White*	Epic 34-74100
46 (April 25, 1992)	6 (May 30, 1992)	20	*In The Closet*	Epic 34-74266
64 (July 11, 1992)	26 (August 8, 1992)	14	*Jam*	Epic 34-74333
53 (July 25, 1992)	3 (March 7, 1992)	20	*Remember The Time*	Epic 34-74200
74 (December 12, 1992)	27 (March 20, 1993)	20	*Heal The World*	Epic 74790
44 (April 10, 1993)	14 (May 15, 1993)	18	*Who Is It*	Epic 74406
63 (July 17, 1993)	7 (September 11, 1993)	20	*Will You Be There (from "Free Willy")*	MJJ/Epic Soundtrax 77060
5 (June 17, 1995)	5 (June 17, 1995)	17	*Scream*****/Childhood (from "Free Willy 2")*	Epic 78000
1 (September 2, 1995)	1 (September 2, 1995)	20	*You Are Not Alone*	Epic 78002
30 (June 8, 1996)	30 (June 8, 1996)	13	*They Don't Care About Us*	Epic 78246
42 (May 10, 1997)	42 (May 10, 1997)	11	*Blood On The Dance Floor*	Epic 78007
91 (August 23, 1997)	91 (August 23, 1997)	2	*Stranger In Moscow*	MJJ 78012
60 (November 17, 2001)	14 (January 26, 2002)	20	*Butterflies*	Epic Album Cut
34 (September 8, 2001)	10 (September 22, 2001)	20	*You Rock My World*	Epic Album Cut
95 (December 6, 2003)	83 (December 13, 2003)	5	*One More Chance*	Epic 76802

US CHART ALBUMS

Week of Entry	Highest Position	Wks	Title	Catalog Number
43 (February 19, 1972)	14 (April 1, 1972)	23	**Got To Be There**	Motown M-747L
119 (August 26, 1972)	5 (November 11, 1972)	32	**Ben**	Motown M-755L
151 (May 5, 1973)	92 (June 23, 1973)	12	**Music And Me**	Motown M-767L
144 (February 15, 1975)	101 (March 15, 1975)	9	**Forever, Michael**	Motown M6-825S1
187 (September 27, 1975)	156 (October 18, 1975)	5	**The Best Of Michael Jackson**	Motown M6-851S1
48 (September 1, 1979)	3 (February 16, 1980)	169	**Off The Wall**	Epic FE 35745
179 (April 25, 1981)	144 (May 30, 1981)	10	**One Day In Your Life**	Motown M8-956M1
11 (December 25, 1982)	1 (February 26, 1983)	122	**Thriller**	Epic QE 38112
104 (June 2, 1984)	46 (July 7, 1984)	15	**Farewell My Summer Love**	Motown 5312
191 (June 23, 1984)	168 (July 21, 1984)	7	**14 Greatest Hits**	Motown 6099
1 (September 26, 1987)	1 (September 26, 1987)	87	**Bad**	Epic 40600
1 (December 14, 1991)	1 (December 14, 1991)	117	**Dangerous**	Epic 45400
1 (July 8, 1995)	1 (July 8, 1995)	36	**HIStory - Past, Present And Future Book I**	Epic E2K 59000
24 (June 7, 1997)	24 (June 7, 1997)	9	**Blood On The Dance Floor: History In The Mix**	MJJ 68000
1 (November 17, 2001)	1 (November 17, 2001)	28	**Invincible**	Epic EK 69400
85 (December 1, 2001)	85 (December 1, 2001)	26	**Greatest Hits: HIStory - Volume 1**	Epic 85250
13 (December 6, 2003)	13 (December 6, 2003)	31	**Number Ones**	MJJ/Epic 88998
154 (December 4, 2004)	154 (December 4, 2004)	1	**The Ultimate Collection**	MJJ/Epic 92600
128 (August 6, 2005)	96 (August 13, 2005)	6	**The Essential Michael Jackson**	Legacy/Epic 94287
191 (July 11, 2009)	139 (August 1, 2009)	3	**Gold**	Motown 011431
195 (July 25, 2009)	95 (July 25, 2009)	1	**The Stripped Mixes**	Motown Digital

UK CHART HISTORY

UK CHART SINGLES

Week of Entry	Highest Position	Wks	Title	Catalog Number
39 (February 12, 1972)	5 (March 4, 1972)	11	**Got To Be There**	Tamla Motown TMG 797
43 (May 20, 1972)	3 (June 24, 1972)	14	**Rockin' Robin**	Tamla Motown TMG 816
41 (August 19, 1972)	8 (September 16, 1972)	11	**Ain't No Sunshine**	Tamla Motown TMG 826
25 (November 25, 1972)	7 (December 9, 1972)	14	**Ben**	Tamla Motown TMG 834
51 (September 15, 1979)	3 (October 20, 1979)	12	**Don't Stop Till You Get Enough**	Epic S EPC 7763
73 (November 24, 1979)	7 (December 15, 1979)	10	**Off The Wall**	Epic S EPC 8045
35 (February 9, 1980)	7 (March 1, 1980)	9	**Rock With You**	Epic S EPC 8206
55 (May 3, 1980)	3 (May 24, 1980)	9	**She's Out Of My Life**	Epic S EPC 8384
53 (July 26, 1980)	41 (August 2, 1980)	5	**Girlfriend**	Epic S EPC 8782
42 (May 23, 1981)	1 (June 27, 1981)	14	**One Day In Your Life**	Motown TMG 976
66 (August 1, 1981)	46 (August 8, 1981)	4	**We're Almost There**	Motown TMG 977
33 (November 6, 1982)	8 (November 20, 1982)	10	**The Girl is Mine****	Epic EPC A2729
57 (January 29, 1983)	1 (March 5, 1983)	15	**Billie Jean**	Epic EPC A 3084
30 (April 9, 1983)	3 (April 23, 1983)	12	**Beat It**	Epic EPC A 3258
38 (June 11, 1983)	8 (June 25, 1983)	9	**Wanna Be Startin' Somethin'**	Epic A 3427
66 (July 23, 1983)	52 (July 30, 1983)	3	**Happy (Love Theme from "Lady Sings The Blues")**	Motown TMG 986

25 (October 15, 1983)	2 (November 19, 1983)	15	*Say Say Say***	Parlophone R 6062
68 (October 15, 1983)	45 (October 22, 1983)	3	*Don't Stop Til You Get Enough*	Record Shack SOHO 10
			(Michael Jackson Medley)	
24 (November 19, 1983)	10 (November 26, 1983)	18	*Thriller*	Epic A 3643
20 (March 31, 1984)	11 (April 7, 1984)	8	*P. Y. T. (Pretty Young Thing)*	Epic A 4136
45 (June 2, 1984)	7 (June 30, 1984)	12	*Farewell My Summer Love*	Motown TMG 1342
62 (August 11, 1984)	33 (September 8, 1984)	8	*Girl You're So Together*	Motown TMG 1355
5 (August 8, 1987)	1 (August 15, 1987)	9	*I Just Can't Stop Loving You****	Epic 650202 7
5 (September 26, 1987)	3 (October 3, 1987)	11	*Bad*	Epic 651155 7
16 (December 5, 1987)	3 (December 12, 1987)	10	*The Way You Make Me Feel*	Epic 651275 7
27 (February 20, 1988)	21 (February 27, 1988)	5	*Man In The Mirror*	Epic 651388 7
31 (April 16, 1988)	8 (May 7, 1988)	9	*I Want You Back '88*	Motown ZB 41913
14 (July 16, 1988)	4 (July 23, 1988)	8	*Dirty Diana*	Epic 651546 7
16 (September 10, 1988)	15 (September 17, 1988)	6	*Another Part Of Me*	Epic 652844 7
12 (November 26, 1988)	8 (December 3, 1988)	10	*Smooth Criminal*	Epic 653026 7
4 (February 25, 1989)	2 (March 4, 1989)	9	*Leave Me Alone*	Epic 654672 7
18 (July 15, 1989)	13 (July 22, 1989)	6	*Liberian Girl*	Epic 654494 7 0
1 (November 23, 1991)	1 (November 23, 1991)	10	*Black Or White*	Epic 6575987
14 (January 18, 1992)	14 (January 18, 1992)	4	*Black Or White*	Epic 6577316
			(Clivilles & Cole Remixes)	
6 (February 15, 1992)	3 (February 22, 1992)	8	*Remember The Time/*	Epic 6577747
			Come Together	
8 (May 2, 1992)	8 (May 2, 1992)	6	*In The Closet*	Epic 6580187
12 (July 25, 1992)	10 (August 1, 1992)	7	*Who Is It*	Epic 6581797
14 (September 12, 1992)	13 (September 19, 1992)	5	*Jam*	Epic 6583606
3 (December 5, 1992)	2 (December 12, 1992)	15	*Heal The World*	Epic 65884885
6 (February 27, 1993)	2 (March 6, 1993)	9	*Give In To Me*	Epic 6590692
11 (July 10, 1993)	9 (July 17, 1993)	8	*Will You Be There*	Epic 6592222
35 (December 18, 1993)	33 (December 25, 1993)	5	*Gone Too Soon*	Epic 6599762
3 (June 10, 1995)	3 (June 10, 1995)	13	*Scream******	Epic 6620222
43 (June 24, 1995)	43 (June 24, 1995)	2	*Scream (4th And 5th Formats)*	Epic 6621277
3 (September 2, 1995)	1 (September 9, 1995)	15	*You Are Not Alone*	Epic 6623102
1 (December 9, 1995)	1 (December 9, 1995)	17	*Earth Song*	Epic 6626955
4 (April 20, 1996)	4 (April 20, 1996)	14	*They Don't Care About Us*	Epic 6629502
2 (August 24, 1996)	2 (August 24, 1996)	9	*Why*	Epic 6636482
4 (November 16, 1996)	4 (November 16, 1996)	11	*Stranger In Moscow*	Epic 6637872
1 (May 3, 1997)	1 (May 3, 1997)	9	*Blood On The Dance Floor*	Epic 6644625
5 (July 19, 1997)	5 (July 19, 1997)	8	*History/Ghosts*	Epic 6647962
2 (October 20, 2001)	2 (October 20, 2001)	15	*You Rock My World*	Epic 6720292
25 (December 22, 2001)	25 (December 22, 2001)	4	*Cry*	Epic 6721822
5 (December 6, 2003)	5 (December 6, 2003)	7	*One More Chance*	Epic 6744805
17 (March 4, 2006)	17 (March 4, 2006)	2	*Don't Stop 'Til You Get Enough*	Epic 82876725112
15 (March 11, 2006)	15 (March 11, 2006)	2	*Rock With You*	Epic 82876725132
11 (March 18, 2006)	10 (July 11, 2009)	5	*Billie Jean*	Epic 82876725172
15 (March 25, 2006)	15 (March 25, 2006)	2	*Beat It*	Epic 82876725182
16 (April 1, 2006)	16 (April 1, 2006)	2	*Bad*	Epic 82876725242
17 (April 8, 2006)	17 (April 8, 2006)	2	*The Way You Make Me Feel*	Epic 82876725252
17 (April 15, 2006)	17 (April 15, 2006)	2	*Dirty Diana*	Epic 82876725272
19 (April 22, 2006)	13 (July 11, 2009)	3	*Smooth Criminal*	Epic 82876725292
15 (April 29, 2006)	15 (April 29, 2006)	2	*Leave Me Alone*	Epic 82876725302
18 (May 6, 2006)	18 (May 6, 2006)	2	*Black Or White*	Epic 82876773302
22 (May 6, 2006)	22 (May 6, 2006)	1	*Jam*	Epic 82876773312
22 (May 13, 2006)	22 (May 13, 2006)	2	*Remember The Time*	Epic 82876773322
20 (May 20, 2006)	20 (May 20, 2006)	2	*In The Closet*	Epic 82876773342
27 (June 3, 2006)	27 (June 3, 2006)	1	*Heal The World*	Epic 82876773382
30 (June 10, 2006)	30 (June 10, 2006)	1	*You Are Not Alone*	Epic 82876773402

		Wks	Title	Catalog Number
34 (June 17, 2006)	33 (July 11, 2009)	1	**Earth Song**	Epic 82876773422
26 (June 24, 2006)	26 (June 24, 2006)	1	**They Don't Care About Us**	Epic 82876773442
22 (July 1, 2006)	22 (July 1, 2006)	1	**Stranger In Moscow**	Epic 82876773462
19 (July 8, 2006)	19 (July 8, 2006)	1	**Blood On The Dance Floor**	Epic 82876773482
57 (November 10, 2007)	12 (July 11, 2009)	1	**Thriller**	Epic 19902989
11 (July 4, 2009)	2 (July 11, 2009)	6	**Man In The Mirror**	Epic 6513886
58 (July 4, 2009)	46 (July 11, 2009)	3	**Ben**	Motown 17200267
72 (July 4, 2009)	57 (July 11, 2009)	2	**Wanna Be Startin' Somethin'**	Epic 18200005
73 (July 4, 2009)	54 (July 11, 2009)	2	**Rock With You**	Epic 82876725132
73 (July 11, 2009)	73 (July 11, 2009)	1	**Off The Wall**	Epic 17900820
51 (July 18, 2009)	51 (July 18, 2009)	1	**Will You Be There**	Epic 10020712
62 (July 18, 2009)	62 (July 18, 2009)	1	**Human Nature**	Epic 19902992
74 (July 18, 2009)	74 (July 18, 2009)	1	**Smile**	Epic 19500015

UK CHART ALBUMS

Week of Entry	Highest Position	Wks	Title	Catalog Number
41 (June 3, 1972)	37 (July 1, 1972)	5	**Got To Be There**	Tamla Motown STML 11205
17 (January 13, 1973)	17 (January 13, 1973)	7	**Ben**	Tamla Motown STML 11220
25 (September 29, 1979)	3 (July 18, 2009)	195	**Off The Wall**	Epic EPC 83468
49 (July 18, 1981)	29 (August 1, 1981)	8	**One Day In Your Life**	Motown STML 12158
62 (June 20, 1981)	11 (August 1, 1981)	18	**The Best Of Michael Jackson**	Motown STMR 9009
29 (December 11, 1982)	1 (March 5, 1983)	207	**Thriller**	Epic EPC 85930
82 (February 12, 1983)	82 (February 12, 1983)	2	**E.T.—The Extra Terrestrial**	MCA 7000
68 (July 9, 1983)	1 (August 20, 1983)	58	**18 Greatest Hits+**	Telstar STAR 2232
97 (December 3, 1983)	66 (December 17, 1983)	3	**9 Singles Pack**	Epic MJ 1
27 (June 9, 1984)	9 (June 23, 1984)	14	**Farewell My Summer Love**	Motown ZL 72227
37 (November 15, 1986)	21 (November 22, 1986)	10	**Their Very Best Back To Back++**	PrioriTyV PTVR 2
1 (September 12, 1987)	1 (September 12, 1987)	117	**Bad**	Epic 4502901
81 (October 31, 1987)	12 (January 2, 1988)	1	**Love Songs**	Telstar STAR 2298
81 (December 26, 1987)	27 (January 9, 1988)	25	**The Michael Jackson Mix**	Stylus SMR 745
91 (July 30, 1988)	91 (July 30, 1988)	1	**Souvenir Singles Pack**	Epic MJ 5
1 (November 30, 1991)	1 (November 30, 1991)	96	**Dangerous**	Epic 4658021
53 (February 29, 1992)	53 (February 29, 1992)	2	**Motown's Greatest Hits**	Motown 5300142
32 (August 15, 1992)	32 (August 15, 1992)	3	**Tour Souvenir Pack**	Epic MJ 4
1 (June 24, 1995)	1 (June 24, 1995)	83	**HIStory—Past, Present And Future, Book I**	Epic 4747091
1 (May 24, 1997)	1 (May 24, 1997)	16	**Blood On The Dance Floor - History In The Mix**	Epic 4875002
7 (July 19, 1997)	5 (July 26, 1997)	9	**The Best Of Michael Jackson - Jackson 5ive - The Motown Years+**	PolyGram TV 5308042
1 (November 10, 2001)	1 (November 10, 2001)	12	**Invincible**	Epic 4951742
68 (November 24, 2001)	15 (March 22, 2003)	16	**Greatest Hits - History Volume 1**	Epic 5018692
1 (November 29, 2003)	1 (November 29, 2003)	56	**Number Ones**	Epic 5138002
75 (December 4, 2004)	75 (December 4, 2004)	1	**The Ultimate Collection**	Epic 5177433
2 (July 30, 2005)	1 (July 11, 2009)	16	**The Essential Michael Jackson**	Epic 5204222
3 (February 23, 2008)	3 (February 23, 2008)	24	**Thriller—25th Anniversary Album**	Epic 88697179862
5 (September 6, 2008)	3 (September 13, 2008)	31	**King Of Pop**	Epic 88697356512
23 (July 11, 2009)	15 (July 18, 2009)	15	**The Very Best Of Michael Jackson & the Jackson 5+**	Universal TV 5308042
5 (July 18, 2009)	4 (July 25, 2009)	4	**The Motown Years+**	Motown 5311546
14 (August 1, 2009)	14 (August 1, 2009)	2	**The Collection**	Epic 88697536212

+ with the Jackson 5   ++ with Diana Ross, Gladys Knight & Stevie Wonder
* with Diana Ross   ** with Paul McCartney   *** with Siedah Garrett   ***** with Janet Jackson

BIBLIOGRAPHY

Crampton, Luke & Dafydd Rees: *Rock & Roll— Year By Year*. Dorling Kindersley, 2003.

IMPRINT

© 2009 TASCHEN GmbH
Hohenzollernring 53, D-50672 Köln
www.taschen.com

Editor: Luke Crampton & Dafydd Rees/Original Media/www.original-media.net
Picture Research: Dafydd Rees & Wellesley Marsh
Editorial Coordination: Florian Kobler and Mischa Gayring, Cologne
Production Coordination: Nadia Najm and Horst Neuzner, Cologne
Design: Sense/Net, Andy Disl and Birgit Eichwede, Cologne
German Translation: Thomas J. Kinne Nauheim
French Translation: Alice Pétillot, Paris
Multilingual Production: Nazire Ergün, Cologne

Printed in Germany
ISBN 978-3-8365-2081-2

To stay informed about upcoming TASCHEN titles, please request our magazine at www.taschen.com/magazine or write to TASCHEN, Hohenzollernring 53, D-50672 Cologne, Germany: contact@taschen.com; Fax: +49-221-254919. We will be happy to send you a free copy of our magazine, which is filled with information about all of our books.

ACKNOWLEDGEMENTS

Victoria Birch, Honey Comer, Ralf Gärtner, Matthew Luts, Joe Medina, Michelle Press, Neal Preston, Jochen Sperber, Kelly Wong

COPYRIGHT